KABBALAH
A Concise Study Guide
Kabbalah Enlightens Our Minds

John Van Auken
Author of *Edgar Cayce and the Kabbalah*

KABBALAH
A Concise Study Guide

Kabbalah Enlightens Our Minds

This 100-page concise study guide is a distillation of the deeper study of Kabbalah in my book, *Edgar Cayce and the Kabbalah: A Resource for Soulful Living*. It goes into much more depth and detail because it is 302 pages long covering more content. It is available on Amazon.com.

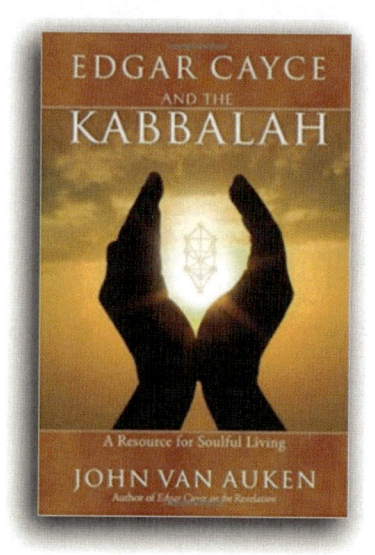

Copyright © 2017 by John Van Auken

ISBN 1974621863

Published by
Living in the Light
P.O. Box 4942
Virginia Beach VA 23454 USA

JohnVanAuken.com
Kabbalah.VanAuken@Gmail.com

Cover Art
"Ezekiel's Vision of God"

Kabbalah Study Guide — Van Auken

Content and Sequence of this Study Guide

INTRODUCTION
SECTION 1
God and the Creation
The Tree of Life and the 10 Emanations
SECTION 2
5 Divisions of Our Being
4 Planes of Existence
7 Heavens
SECTION 3
Angels, Archangels, Demons
Incantations and Talismans
The Meaning of Numbers
SECTION 4
Ecstasy of God Consciousness
Spiritualizing Body, Mind, and Soul

Proverbs 4:5-9

- "Get *wisdom*, get *understanding*. Forget it not; neither decline from the words of my mouth. Forsake her not, and she shall preserve thee. Love her, and she shall keep thee. *Wisdom* is the principal thing; therefore get *wisdom*. And with all thy getting get *understanding*. Exalt her, and she shall promote thee. She shall bring thee to honor, when thou dost embrace her. She shall give to your head an ornament of grace, a *crown* of glory shall she deliver to thee.

Copyright 2010 © by John Van Auken

Kabbalah Study Guide – Van Auken

Special Note

Throughout this study I will include other sources of wisdom and enlightenment, including Patanjali's *Yoga Sutras*, Gnostic teachings, mystical Christianity (Jesus was Jewish) and Edgar Cayce's visions into the mystical teachings that naturally complement the Kabbalah vision. These other sources add much to our understanding.

INTRODUCTION

Kabbalah, or Qabalah, comes from the Hebrew word QBLH (there are no vowels in the language), which is derived from the root QBL, meaning "to receive," but with the nuance "to correspond" in a manner that is "face to face"—as Moses received from God, and communicated with God face to face, such that his face "shone" from the experience. (Exodus 34:29) The term is sometimes written Qabalah and Cabala, but better reflects its origin and sounding when written in English as Kabbalah—pronounced *ka-bal'-lah* and *kab-ba-lah'*. Most Westerners pronounce it *ka-bal'-lah*, because of the word *cabal* (of French origin), meaning a group of persons secretly involved in artifices and intrigue. Legend holds that Kabbalah was first taught by God to a select group of angels. Then, after the fall of the angels (which is explained in Week 3), Kabbalah was taught to humans—many of whom were the fallen angels (more on this later). The wisdom was then passed along through Adam, Enoch, Moses, Jacob, Joseph, Elijah, Ezekiel, and Daniel, and traveled from Eden to Egypt, the ancient land of mysteries. Here the knowledge spread beyond the initial group to many others, even non-Jews, who made it their own, adding their perspectives and experiences to the wisdom. As a result of this there are variations of Kabbalistic teachings. I have gathered together the teachings that most closely reflect original wisdom, and in some cases those that most closely reflective of God's repetitive message over ages of the spiritual enlightenment of humanity.

From ancient times, Kabbalah was carried forward orally and secretly, only select souls were initiated into this training and practice. Then, in the Middle Ages, its elements (recorded and legendary) were finally codified in various texts and distributed as the mystical, esoteric books growing out of Judaism. However, it was never a part of traditional Judaism. Also, many mystical Christians had copies of these texts, and developed their own versions. The main manuscripts that make up the body of Kabbalah wisdom listed in the illustration on page 6. Many of these texts didn't initially exist in one binding, but were fragmented writings or pamphlets that were later compiled into various books. Unlike the Bible, Koran, and Vedas, there is no single book titled *The Kabbalah*. As we study together we will touch on portions of each of these classical Kabbalistic texts.

Kabbalah is not a single book like the Bible or Koran; it is a collection of ancient and classical manuscripts. Here's a list:

The Book of Creation (*Sefer Yetzirah*)
The Book of the Splendor (*Sefer ha-Zohar*) or simply Zohar
The Mystery of the Chariot (*Ma'aseh Merkabah*)
The Mystery of the Beginning (*Ma'aseh Bereshit*)
The Book of the Brightness (*Sefer ha-Bahir*)
The Book of the Angel (*Sefer Raziel*)
Life in the World to Come (*Chayye Olam Ha Ba*)

Kabbalah Study Guide – Van Auken

The Mystery of the Chariot was among the earliest writings in Jewish mysticism. It was based on a vision experienced by the prophet Ezekiel. While standing by a river in Babylon, Ezekiel saw a vision in the heavens of four winged creatures, spinning wheels, and a fiery throne. Seated on the throne was "the glory of the Lord." (Ezekiel I) These earliest Kabbalists used this vision as a way of describing the realms of God, which are above the material reality that humans know. The early mystics meditated on the image of the fiery chariot, using it as a visual mantra. They described the path through the upper world to the heavenly chariot as dangerous and terrifying. It led past seven palaces filled with armies of angels. Rivers of fire flowed out of the sky as angels drew the chariot through the air. The goal of meditating on the chariot was to overcome the obstacles en route to the chariot itself and see the image of the Lord seated on the throne. Reaching the throne required extensive spiritual training, tremendous focus and concentration, and a deeply founded desire to know God. This early book introduces the idea of the ecstasy that comes from direct communion with God on a physical and emotional level. (More on this in the chapter on ecstasy.) This notion of communication with God forms the core of all Kabbalistic thought. *The Mystery of the Chariot* also introduces the idea that close encounters with God could be dangerous to untrained minds. Though the Torah indicates that any faithful Jews could communicate directly with God without risk, Kabbalists believed that contact with a force as infinite and omnipotent as God could lead to madness. For this reason, Kabbalists initially limited study of Kabbalah to married men over forty who had studied the Torah and the Talmud.

The Mystery of the Beginning developed from a mystical interpretation of the first chapters of Genesis, in which God created the universe and all the life within it. *The Mystery of the Beginning* explained that because God encompasses *all* of creation, humans are by default a part of God. Rather than merely accepting the biblical account of creation, Kabbalists read meaning into every word of the Torah. They would ask questions like, "What is implied by Eve coming from out of Adam?" This penetrating, mystical interpretation of Genesis led Kabbalists to form their own account of creation, and this became apparent with the publishing of *The Mystery of the Beginning*. Their account differed significantly from the traditional Jewish understanding of the origins of the universe, revealing a growing contrast between traditional Judaism and Kabbalism.

The Book of Creation is a short book that expands on the theories in *The Mystery of the Beginning*. *The Book of Creation* proposes that God created the world with thirty-two secret paths of wisdom. These paths of wisdom are composed of the ten emanations (sefirot) and the twenty-two letters of the Hebrew alphabet. The first chapter of *The Book of Creation* explains the emanations – and this is the first time this concept of Divine emanations appears in Jewish literature. However, the emanations of *The Book of Creation* differ from the ten "aspects of God" that appear much later in Kabbalistic thought. Here they take the form of numbers with mystical qualities, each one representing a stage of creation and a pathway from and back to God. The Torah tends to personify God as a humanlike being who can talk and interact with people on earth – the familiar image of an old bearded man in the sky. *The Book of Creation* presents God as an unknowable, genderless force entirely devoid of form or emotion. In the Torah, God creates simply by using the power of his word, his command. But in *The Book of Creation*, God creates through emanations, or projections of its being. God becomes a part of the universe, everywhere and nowhere at once, a spirit with infinite power. This initial mystical theory – that the world was created through emanations of the Divinity – forms the foundation of Kabbalistic thought and separates it further from traditional Judaism. This concept also created much controversy.

Everything about the emanations – from where they came from to what they mean – has been debated for many hundreds of years.

The Book of Brightness begins with a discussion of *The Book of Creation*, and the second part is an attempt to clarify the order of the emanations, which *The Book of Creation* describes as ten numbers. In *The Book of Brightness* the emanations are described for the first time as attributes of God's being. In addition to representing a particular part of God, each emanation also corresponds to a stage in creation and a character from the Bible. Another concept that *The Book of Brightness* introduces for the first time is the Tree of Life, a visual representation of the ten emanations. *The Book of Brightness* describes the locations of each emanation on the Tree of Life. The Tree is intended to symbolize the body of "Adam Kadmon," also known as "primordial man," a prototype for the creation of human beings. Adam Kadmon is not the Adam of Adam and Eve in Genesis, but a kind of mystical template for human beings that God made before creating them. He is proof that our being was created in God's image. Like the Word or Logos that Adam Kadmon represents, we are a part of God. The Tree of Life was considered to reflect the body of Adam, and the spiritual form of God linked symbolically in visual diagrams of the ten emanations. Kabbalah is in many ways a spiritual movement that is both thorough and obscure! As Kabbalists tried to unravel the mysteries of the universe, such as creation and the birth of humankind, they argued for centuries over passages in the Torah. The closer they looked at words, the more mysterious the universe became. Though exceptionally difficult, *The Book of Brightness* arranged and organized Kabbalah's sprawling ideas into a coherent form in one volume. Most important, it explained that the emanations are aspects of God's being, not just numbers. The emanations represent God's attributes, such as wisdom, mercy, and beauty, and Kabbalists believe they represent the core components to having a fulfilling life.

Today the *Zohar* is the most popular book of the Kabbalah. In 1280 CE, a Spanish mystic named Moses de Leon began circulating small booklets written in archaic Aramaic, an ancestral language to the Hebrew and Arabic alphabets. De Leon claimed that the booklets were taken from ancient texts written by the great second-century rabbi Simeon ben Yohai. Rabbi Yohai, fleeing persecution by the Romans in Palestine, hid in a cave for thirteen years with his son, Eliezar. Legend has it that Elijah actually visited Yohai and his son in the cave, after which God inspired Yohai to write down the wisdom he gathered from Elijah's teachings. De Leon claimed his pamphlets contained Yohai's writing. Kabbalists believed de Leon's story for hundreds of years. However, today some researchers believe de Leon wrote the pamphlets himself. The strongest argument against this is that de Leon was not a deeply spiritual man who was practicing deep meditative communion with God, and was not a spiritually inspired poetic writer. The *Zohar* is poetic mystical wisdom, written in a style considered to be "automatic writing," or "creative writing," with the Spirit inspiring the writer. This type of writing requires the writer to enter a mystical trance and write what comes to mind, no matter how scattered or unrelated. It is believed that this type of writing reaches through the veils of lower consciousness, allowing higher levels, even God's consciousness, to come through. Others contend that bizarre style of the *Zohar* results *not* from the automatic writing, but from the contributions of *several* writers over hundreds of years.

The *Zohar* describes the journey of Rabbi Simeon ben Yohai and ten companions through Galilee, the northern region of Palestine and, formerly, the kingdom of Israel. Along their journey, the travelers discuss their interpretations of the Torah, and specifically the Torah's main characters. The characters become a part of the narrative of the *Zohar*, their lives weaving in and out of those of Yohai and his group. The companions come and go gracefully within their own group, turning from one character to another. The *Zohar* uses the term "Ein Sof" for God, meaning the "Infinite Eternal." Ein Sof is a departure from the traditional concept of divinity, which portrays God as a knowable presence, a being in the heavens that people can comprehend and feel. Ein Sof is so vast that it's unknowable, beyond the boundaries of human comprehension. Kabbalists believe that at most they can know merely fragments of the Infinite Eternal (Ein Sof), which they receive only through profound mystical experiences. The *Zohar* depicts God as a distant presence that sacrificed Its own preeminence in order to create the universe.

Though the *Zohar* and its teachings spread quickly from Spain and Italy into other parts of Western Europe, it was slow to reach Eastern Europe – at least at first. After the expulsion of the Jews from Spain in 1492, study of the *Zohar* became more widespread as Jews fled eastward. The *Zohar* remains in print today and has been translated into English in a twenty-two-volume set.

In addition to these volumes, there are over a hundred texts elaborating on Kabbalistic concepts and practices. And even though we have these Kabbalah codices, wisdom is still sought and received directly from heaven through revelation, intuitive perception, prayerful communion with the Divine, various forms of deep meditation, and even spontaneous enlightenment. The literature of the *Hekhalot* movement (literally, *heavenly palaces* or *temples of God*, containing stories of journeys to heaven) and the *Merkabah* movement (developed from Ezekiel's vision of the chariot of God, from Hebrew *RKB*, "to ride" to heaven), describes in detail how seekers enter meditative-like trance states in order to commune with God. Many believe that God still speaks to the minds and hearts of those open to learning and following a more spiritual way of living. Yet, intuitive "receiving" often comes after one has been studying and practicing the written knowledge in daily life. It often happens in moments of quiet reflection, an inner awareness sparks a communion, even if only for a fleeting moment. But one can go with the energy and enlightenment of these moments for a very long time.

I've divided our study into 4 one-week study sessions. We begin with God and the Creation, and then the 10 Emanations from God into our manifested realm of existence. Both in the microcosm of our body/mind world and outside in the macrocosm of Universe. We'll study the famous Kabbalah "Tree of Life" that contains the 10 Emanations. At times you may feel that we are getting "way out there" and far from practical aspects of living our life today in this reality. And such a feeling is genuine and should be honored. Balancing the esoteric with exoteric is all important to sanity and well-being. We are human AND divine. And both need their exercise! Therefore, our study here is important for stretching our minds and elevating the vibrations of our bodies. It is good to stretch from finite, individual awareness and activity to infinite, universal vibes and awareness. We need to touch our immortal self and the realms that our souls will have to live in beyond this incarnation. And that is what this course is about! Enlightening our minds and souls to a greater reality and our ultimate destiny by building a better understanding of our origin, journey, and destiny. From Genesis to Revelation is the path of this course. But it does not run in a straight line, rather it moves around a bit – touching here and there as we expand our minds and raise our vibrations. I will be your attentive mentor. I read every post and respond to those that I feel I can add something to or adjust a perspective that is not quite inline with pure Kabbalistic teaching. Sometimes (and I emphasize "sometimes") I will even respond to off-topic issues that arise as we go on – such as dreams, meditative experiences, and the like.

Kabbalah Study Guide – Van Auken
SECTION I PART I
God and the Creation

"In the beginning God created the heavens and the earth. The earth was waste and void (remember this); and darkness was upon the face of the deep (remember this); and the spirit of God moved upon the face of the waters (remember this). And God said, "Let there be light; and there was light." –Genesis 1:1-3

In the above quote from Genesis it is important for us to grasp important statements in this opening that give us insight into the beginning, the creation, and the nature of existence. And those are:

1. There are two fundamental realms: heavens (plural) and earth.
2. The earth was "void," meaning "nothing," "empty," and "vacuum." Thus it was a thought not yet a thing.
3. Darkness was upon the "deep" is a key for our minds to use in seeking reunion with our Creator, who exists in the unseen "deep." This is the womb of God: dark and deep and the source of life. Again, it is a state of consciousness not a thing.
4. "The SPIRIT of God moved" reveals the ultimate nature of God. As Jesus taught: "God is a Spirit." (John 4:24)
5. What waters? The earth was void. Cayce's readings teach that the condition of "water" reveals the three conditions of our own existence: solid (physical), liquid (mental-emotional), and vapor/cloud (spiritual). God moved on the face of our original mental-emotional condition and said: "Let there be light." Here's were we touch our original moment of enlightened awareness. Cayce's readings teach that "the light" was the light of consciousness — we became conscious! Now notice that the earth is not yet a physical thing. All of this occurred in the Mind of God. This is very important to our enlightenment. Real life exists in the mind. Thoughts are as real as things. After the physical death of our bodies we exist as a mental beings, minds. We are minds living inside physical vessels. Our minds have three levels: conscious, subconscious, and superconscious.

The following is about Kabbalah's view of God. It may be a bit too esoteric for you but try to "feel" the gist of what they are attempting to convey to us about the Source and Container of All Life. As you're reading this keep in mind that Edgar Cayce taught that the "unseen forces" and the "universal forces" have more of an impact on us than we realize. And if we could come to some little sense of the Infinite inside our finite being, then we'd do so much better than just living completely focused on physical, personality life.

GOD
And Creation

The "Ein Sof" means the "Infinite Eternal"

"In the beginning God [Elohim] created the heavens and the earth. The earth was waste and void; and darkness was upon the face of **the deep**; and the **spirit of God** moved upon the face of the waters. And God said, Let there be **light**; and there was light." –Genesis 1:1-3

Ein Sof Aur is "Limitless Light"

Copyright 2010 © by John Van Auken

In Kabbalah, God is not a being. He is not a big bearded man in the sky. He is not even a man. Cayce taught that Jesus was the man, Christ was the Spirit within the man. And Jesus told us that of himself he did nothing but what the Spirit within him showed him. From the perspective of the Jewish Kabbalists, God is the transcendent reality of consciousness and energy that is within all exists. This is reflected in the descriptive identity the Kabbalists have given to God: Ein Sof. Ein roughly means "without" or "void" or "empty"; Ein Sof roughly means "without end," but is better interpreted as "Infinite Eternal"; conveying its condition is beyond space and time: spacially infinite and timelessly eternal. Ein Sof Aur means "Infinite Eternal Light"; light conveys its quality of consciousness, that being "illuminated." You and I want an illuminated consciousness, and contact with the Infinite Eternal Light naturally results in lighting up our finite minds.

Again, the opening paragraph of the Bible hints at this:

"In the beginning the Infinite Eternal (God) created the heavens and the earth. The earth was waste and void; and darkness was upon the face of the deep; and the spirit of God moved upon the face of the waters. And God said, 'Let there be light'; and there was light. " –Genesis Genesis 1:1-3

Keep in mind that Cayce's readings teach this "light" was the light of consciousness. And from Kabbalah we learn that "The deep" is an important "location" on the Tree of Life and is a "disposition" of consciousness or "state" of consciousness. We can find it in introspection, deep prayer, meditation, and dreams. It will eventually help us experience oneness with the Infinite Eternal (Ein Sof).

The Scriptures begin in Hebrew, *breshit bara elohim* [there is no distinction between lower case and upper case letters in Hebrew], which translated into English as: "In the beginning God...." The first name for God, as seen is this first line of Genesis, is Elohim. It is a plural Hebrew word that may be interpreted as "the Deities," and the verse about creating us is translated in the plural as well: "Let us make man in our image, after our likeness." (Genesis 1:26) By using the plural form, the authors were likely attempting to convey the collective nature of the Creator; to keep us from thinking that God was a divine individual projecting individuals in its image, and keep us from thinking that God is a separate being from us. Rather, it is a collective consciousness within which all of the creation was conceived and exists. Elohim may be likened to the "great assembly" spoke of in Psalm 82:1, indicating all exists within this collective. Here's that line in the Psalm: "God is in the assembly of God; he is judging among the gods." Curiously though, when this plural name is used, it is commonly construed with singular verbs and adjectives, adding to the belief that this is not polytheism but the all-inclusive collective nature of God. Before we leave this Psalm, consider verse 6, "I said, 'You are gods, all of you are sons [and daughters] of the Most High.'" This is clearly a reference to our highest level of being, our Spirit Being and Spirit Mind created in the image of God (more on this in the lesson on divisions of our being).

As we have just read, Kabbalah uses another name for the highest of God's qualities, a name that does not appear in any Scriptures. Ein Sof (Infinite Eternal) relates more to God's vast mind that is beyond the visible creation. This is God's purest essence, meaning "the infinite, eternal" realm of life (*ad le-ein sof*). Ein Sof does not appear in any of the Scriptures or Rabbinic writings. Gershom Scholem (1897-1982), widely regarded as the founder of the modern, academic study of Kabbalah, became the first Professor of Jewish Mysticism at the Hebrew University of Jerusalem. He taught that Ein Sof is the Emanator of the emanations (*sefirot*) found in the Tree of Life. Emanations are God's energy and consciousness flowing throughout the creation, which we will study in detail later.

As the creation progresses, the name of God is changed. These name changes reflect changes in our relationship to God, not God's changing condition. God is unchanged. But we change as we use our free wills and journey through life. Originally, we were created in God's image, in Elohim's image. (Genesis 1:26) Then, in chapter two, *Yahweh Elohim* (interpreted in English as "Lord God") creates us out of the dust of the earth and breathes the breath of life into us. (Genesis 2:7) In Chapter four, *Yahweh* (just the "Lord") is used during and after the birth of Cain and Abel. As the Bible continues God is called *Adonai* (Master), *El* (Mighty One), *El 'Elyon* (Most High God), *El Shaddai* (God Almighty), *El 'Olam* (Everlasting God), *El Hai* (Living God), and *Avinu* ("Our Father" — as found in Isaiah 63:16; Jeremiah 31:9; Psalms 103:13; 1 Chronicles 29:10, pronounced *a-vee'-new*). In the New Testament, Jesus continues the Jewish concept of God as Father, using *Abba* ("Father" in Aramaic and in colloquial Hebrew at the time of Jesus) and ho pater ("The Father" in Greek).

All of these names reveal our shifting relationship with God as we grow away or toward oneness with our Creator. Consider how God identified Him-Herself to Moses on the mount when answering Moses' question about His name: "I am that I am." (Exodus 3:13-14) "And Moses said unto God, 'Behold, when I come unto the children of Israel, and shall say unto them, the God of your fathers hath sent me unto you; and they shall say to me, What is his name? What shall I say unto them? And God said unto Moses, 'I AM THAT I AM'; and he said, 'Thus shalt thou say unto the children of Israel, I AM hath sent me unto you.'"

We may read this as indicating that the collective cannot be separated from the creation; therefore, the sense of self that we feel when we say or think "I am," is a portion of the great I AM in whose image all of the little "I am's" were created and exist. Our "I am" is an aspect of the great "I AM." This is where it gets a little challenging since our minds are mostly finite. We feel individualized in a specific body in a specific location and time. Despite this feeling, a portion of us is ALWAYS in the

Infinite Consciousness of our Creator. And with the slightest shift in our minds, we can become aware of our infinite existence while still being expressed finitely. It's a paradox — a paradox that is difficult for our normal, daily minds to perceive, but NOT impossible. And that is what Kabbalah wants to help us do.

Let's take a spin through the creation story. Actually we're going to go to "before the creation"! The reason for this is that it is believed that this will touch a deep memory within us that was there — yes, there "before the beginning"! As strange as this sounds it is true. Let's just let go of our present perspective on reality and take a little imaginative journey.

Edgar Cayce 262-86

"When you say Creative Force, God, Jehovah, Yahweh, Abba, what do you mean? In the various phases of your own consciousness—or of those who in their activities seek, as you (if you seek aright)—seek to be one *with* Him yet to *know* self to *be* self, *I am*, in and with the GREAT I AM."

THE CREATION

The Kabbalah and Cayce tell a curious creation story. It goes something like this: Before anything existed, there was nothing—absolutely nothing. Emptiness was everywhere and there was no place any where. Vast emptiness was everywhere. Only infinite emptiness and absolute stillness existed. This was the condition of the Creator before the Creation. How then could the creation occur? How could something come from out of nothing? This is the mystery and the difficulty with our seeking to know God, to know the almost unknowable. However, if we think of this pre-creation condition as a consciousness — an infinite, universal consciousness that was perfectly still, with no thoughts — then we can see how it could be empty and yet possess all the power to conceived. It's just like our mind with no thoughts: quiet, empty, still. We may think of this infinite consciousness as the womb of our Mother's Mind. And just as our mind would conceive thoughts, images, and movements, so the Infinite Consciousness began to conceive the entire creation! The thought of light, which brought stars, which brought galaxies, and on and on, eventually sunlight on water running over pebbles in a stream. The creation spun out from its empty Source filling the universe with life.

What were some of the initial expressions of the infinite, universal mind? Well, at one moment there arose the *will* to create. This is the Divine Will motivated to create. Therefore, two of our Creator's qualities are Will and Creativity. And since we were eventually created in our Creator's image, these two qualities are within us! Each of us has will and creativity.

Our Hidden Creator

The Kabbalah teaches that the Infinite Emptiness (Mother's Womb) had to make room for the creation, so a portion of the pre-creation Creator retreated into an unknowable, unreachable "place." This move kept the original purity secure from whatever happens during the flow of creative life. This is true in the Infinite AND in our little finite SOUL. Cayce teachings that within each of us is a pure, untouched sanctuary that has not been tainted by whatever we've done with our free will. (I was happy to hear this when I first read it. It gave me a joy my inner child was untainted by my mistakes.)

After the pure was hidden and secure, the creation exploded! The Big Bang of Life burst forth! And Kabbalah helps us understand the initial energies and original patterns through the Ten Emanations that reflect the nature of the invisible, infinite Creator into the visible reality. The Emanations are in the macrocosm of the entire universe and in the microcosm of our individual being. They are within us, and around us, and flow through us. They are seen in the outer reality in a reflective manner, allowing us to intuit their unseen nature. And, best of all, we can awaken to them and use them to illuminate and energize our bodies, minds, and souls.

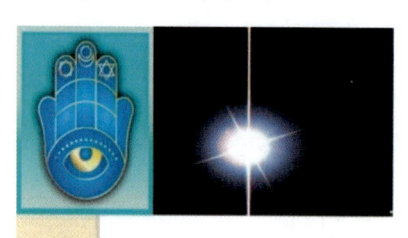

GOD And Creation

The Infinite Eternal is Hidden

According to Kabbalah, God, being perfect, needed to withdrawal to a hidden "empty place" in order for the evolving creation to progress freely—because it would contain imperfections and mistakes would occurred. Since God is perfect—needed to withdraw.

Copyright 2010 © by John Van Auken

Living out here in the seen creation, we would be wiser and stronger if we opened our hearts and minds to the *unseen* Creative Forces and harmonized our will with the flow of the Creator's will.

God, Creation, and the Planes of Existence

The Kabbalah creation is explained in the following mystical manner, and the best way for you to get something out of this is allow your mind to imagine or "feel" these formless conditions and forces. Be imaginative, as the child within you was so early in this life!

Mystical, Esoteric Creation

Within the unbounded womb of "Infinite Nothingness," that which is the essence of "Infinite Something" moved, expressing itself in a burst of "Light Without Limit." This light is both consciousness and luminescence. "Infinite Nothingness" is Ein, also spelled En and Ayn, and is comparable to Gnosticism's "the Depth" and "Non-Being God" (*ouk on theos*) as well as "Unknown God" (*hagnostos theos*). "Infinite Something" is *Ein Sof*, also spelled *Ein Soph*, En Soph, and Ayn Sof, and is comparable to

Gnosticism's "Fullness of Being" (*bythos pleroma*). "Light Without Limit" is *Ein Sof Aur*, possibly comparable to Gnosticism's "First Father" (*propator*).

The "Infinite Something" (Ein Sof) emanated ten aspects of itself and twenty-two channels of energy. The Infinite's expression flowed outward to four concentric planes of consciousness. We will study the four planes in detail in a later lesson.

The Primordial Being or Prototype of Beingness

There is a variation on this brief description which teaches that the Infinite conceived of Primordial Being first, and subsequently the Primordial Being (or prototype) conceived all the subsequent beings (you and me). This is comparable to Gnosticism's idea that First Father conceived the central Monad (*monas*), an indivisible oneness that pervades all life, seen and unseen. This Monad is comparable to the Logos, the Word—as the disciple John wrote: "In the beginning was the Word, and the Word was with God, and the Word was God. All things were made through this One." There is a First Source (*proarche*), which may be compared to Edgar Cayce's "First Cause." In Gnosticism humankind (*anthropos*) came out of the indivisible oneness of the Monad. In Kabbalah, humankind came out of the first being, *Adam Kadmon* (the Logos, the prototype of beingness).

Believe me I know how other-worldly, ethereal, and just plain "far out" this all sounds upon first reading it! Hang in with me and you'll begin to grasp the unseen depth in these expressions and seemingly impractical ideas that can't possibly relate to our lives here, today. This is why rabbis have always said no one should study Kabbalah until they've lived enough of this life to be open to the more expanded life of a spirit being in the unseen forces and dimensions of the greater life. After a few more days you should come back to this page and read it slowly again. I found that with each reading I gained some new awareness of the message it carries. Also, the subsequent weeks will add clarity to this, and then reading it again will make more sense.

SECTION 1 PART 2
10 Emanations and The Tree of Life

NOTE: Please don't let yourself get overwhelmed by the following. Just read it as a curiosity. Your deeper self sees through the same eyes as you, and it will get the value of this often strange and complex information.

Introduction

The Infinite Eternal (*Ein Sof*) reveals its nature through ten emanations (*sefirot*) that form the Tree of Life. These emanations reflect attributes of the Infinite Eternal that reveal the infinite, unseen Divinity's energy, consciousness, and qualities. The life force of the Infinite Eternal flows from the hidden Creator throughout the observable creation in a specific pattern depicted in the Tree of Life. The emanations and the Tree are the mystical "image of God" (*tzelem Elokim*; also *tselem Elohim*). Since we were created in the image of God (Genesis 1:26), the emanations and the Tree reveal how we are constructed and how the Life Energy flows through us. Think of the Tree is like a map of the macrocosm of the universe and the microcosm within us. Our spiritual journey into existence and back to reunion with the Creator follows according to the Tree. Think of the emanations as metaphysical orbs of the Divinity's energy, consciousness, and qualities that we can come to know and imbue our whole being.

The origin of the term *sefirot* (plural of *sefirah*, sometimes written *sephiroth* or *shephirah*) remains a mystery of antiquity. The Hebrew word SPHR (remember, there are no vowels in the language) means "to form," especially to form in a sphere or orb. Some writers point out that this term is akin to the ancient Egyptian term *khefer*, also meaning "to form," but in the context of the sacred Egyptian beetle, *Khephra* or *Khefra*, it relates to rolling the dung of carnal, physical life into a ball and toward the rising sun in the morning, planting a seed in the dung ball, and by the heat of high noon new life awakens—symbolizing resurrection from the dung of material life by cooperating with the Sun or Ra, the Sun god, seen as the source of light and life. This indicates that the spheres or orbs on the Tree of Life enliven and enlighten us so that we may resurrect to life we originally had with God in the Garden of Eden and the Heavens.

Some writers believe sefirah refers to numbering rather than forming spheres. Thus, the emanations reflect the sequence of their formation and their rank. Whatever the case, each sefirah is an orb and a number representing an energy, a consciousness, a vibration, and a disposition.

The word sefirah may also mean, in some contexts, "to write" and "to speak," associated with the word *lesaper*, "to express," "to communicate." Thus the emanations are an expression, a communication from the Infinite Eternal to the created, from our Creator to us.

Kabbalah Study Guide — Van Auken

These emanations are comparable to Gnosticism's aions, syzygies, sonships, and light kings. In Gnosticism, all emanations are paired; in Kabbalah, only six of the ten emanations are paired: Wisdom with Understanding, Mercy with Judgment, and Victory with Splendor.

Kabbalah teaches that when the Creation burst forth from the darkness of the deep, it did so with such intense brilliance, awesome power, and extreme velocity that it broke wide open all the orbs (*shevirat ha-keilim*: "breaking of the vessels"). The orbs were unable to contain the Light (*netzotzot*)—that is, all except the tenth orb: called the "Kingdom" and the little "I am" of those created in the image of the Great I AM. Wonderfully the contained Light then flowed backward to its Creator, gathering all the shards (*kelipot*) of the broken orbs and repairing them! Miraculously the image of God as expressed in the Tree of Life was whole again for all of creation to comprehend.

Tree of Life

Here are illustrations of the Tree of Life with two variations on the naming of the orbs of emanations. Think of them as expressions of God's essence. One is traditional and the other is more mystical, often taught in secret.

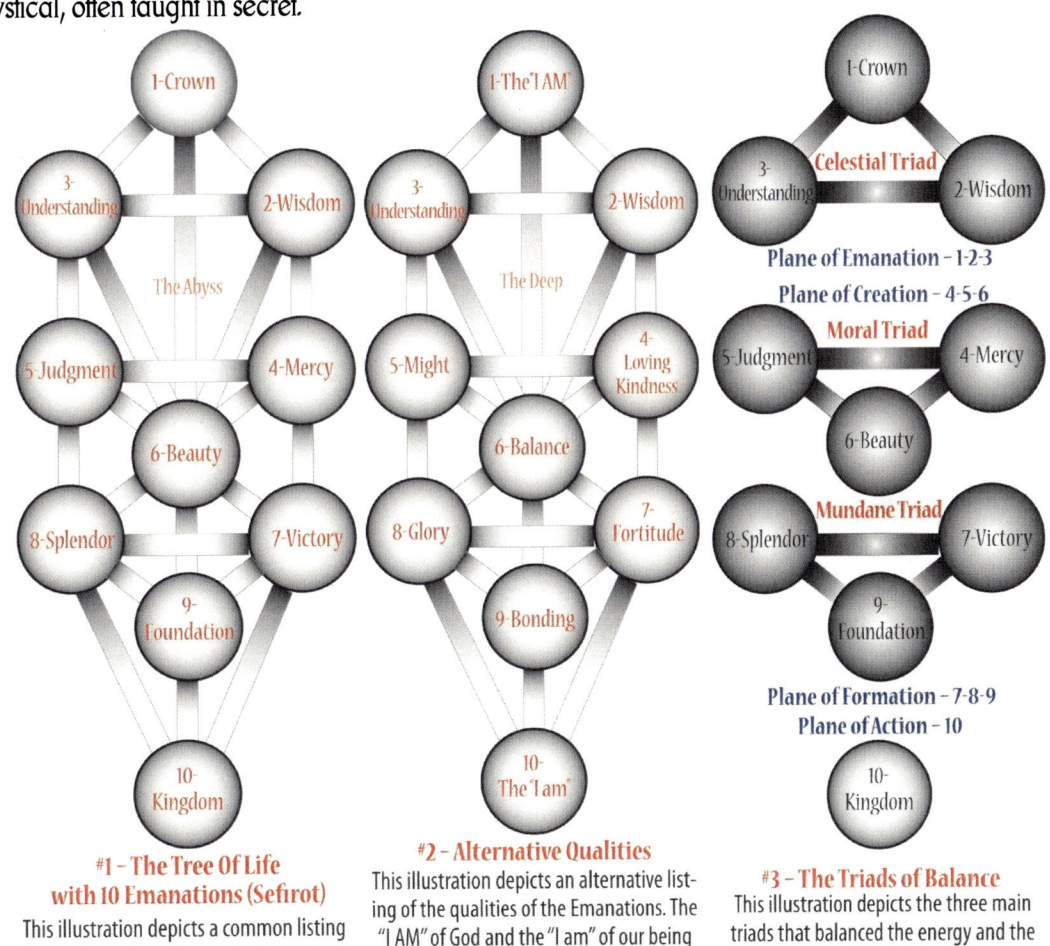

#1 – The Tree Of Life with 10 Emanations (Sefirot)
This illustration depicts a common listing of the order and qualities of the Emanations.

Emanations: 1-Crown, 2-Wisdom, 3-Understanding, The Abyss, 4-Mercy, 5-Judgment, 6-Beauty, 7-Victory, 8-Splendor, 9-Foundation, 10-Kingdom

#2 – Alternative Qualities
This illustration depicts an alternative listing of the qualities of the Emanations. The "I AM" of God and the "I am" of our being are destined for reunion.

Emanations: 1-The "I AM", 2-Wisdom, 3-Understanding, The Deep, 4-Loving Kindness, 5-Might, 6-Balance, 7-Fortitude, 8-Glory, 9-Bonding, 10-The "I am"

#3 – The Triads of Balance
This illustration depicts the three main triads that balanced the energy and the four Planes of Existence.

- **Celestial Triad** — Plane of Emanation – 1-2-3
- **Moral Triad** — Plane of Creation – 4-5-6
- **Mundane Triad** — Plane of Formation – 7-8-9
- Plane of Action – 10

Before the repair, chaos reigned. As the Light flowed backward, order was reestablished. The Infinite was now revealed in a balanced manner. According to Kabbalah, this balance was achieved

Kabbalah Study Guide – Van Auken

by "hinging" energies and perspectives that appeared to be opposing forces, but in the balance, they complemented one another in specific triads, or trinities.

Three primary, triangular balances were created. In the Celestial Triad contains the Godhead of the great "I AM" (emanation 1: Crown) held in balance the "Father of Fathers" (emanation 2: Wisdom) and the "Mother of Mothers" (emanation 3: Understanding). In the Moral Triad contains Beauty (emanation 6) held in balance Mercy (emanation 4) and Judgment (emanation 5). And, in the Mundane Triad contains Foundation (emanation 9) held in balance Splendor (emanation 8) and Victory (emanation 7).

With all of these repaired, in balance, fully illuminated, energized, and conscious, the Light and Life flowed evenly throughout the creation—from the Creator to the created and back again. All was in balance and in harmonic motion.

Remember, this is both in the infinity of the cosmos and in the finite realm of our being.

From a Kabbalistic perspective, "sin" is a separation of a portion of the Tree of Life from the whole. When this happens, the flow is broken, the balance lost. To restore health and well-being, reunion must be achieved. This reunion includes the re-balancing of the energy, consciousness, and qualities of the orb that has been separated.

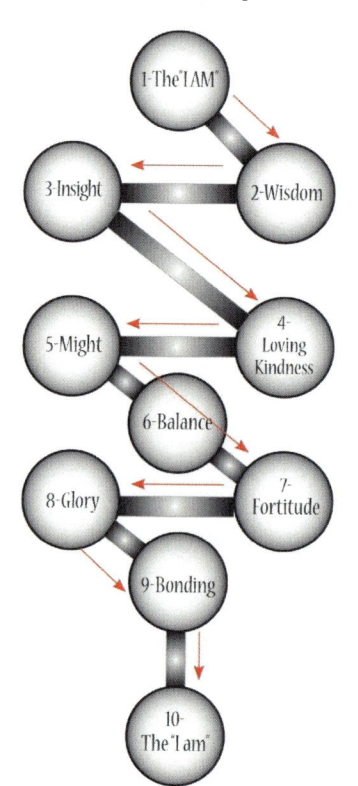

#4 - The Flow of the Emanation
This illustration depicts the flow of energy *from* God and *returning* to God, moving between the I AM and the I am.

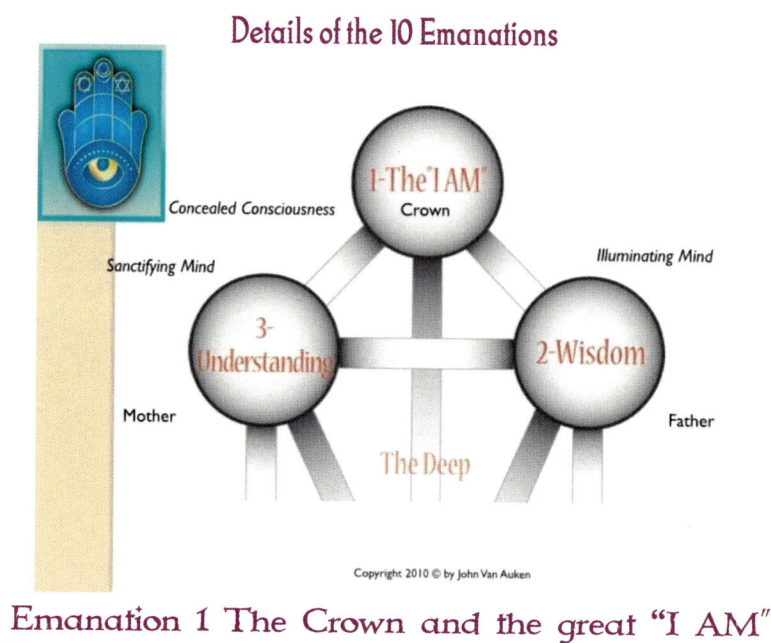

Details of the 10 Emanations

Emanation 1 The Crown and the great "I AM"

The first emanation is the Crown, the "I AM" of the "I am that I am." (Exodus 3:14) It is the emanation of the unseen Creator as the Godhead, the biblical "Most High" God. The Creator's Essence emerged from "the deep" (Genesis 1:2) as a light piercing the endless darkness—the first brilliant, shining orb, out of which the remaining emanations emerged. The plan of the entire universe is contained in this first emanation. The concept of unity amid diversity was born and is maintained here.

Some Kabbalists believe the first emanation "shields" the physical universe and the creation from the blinding Light of the original Creative Spirit. In this mission it is considered to be the Concealed Consciousness, veiled from manifested life. Some believe it is unknowable. Others teach that it is indeed knowable but only after one has ascended to a much higher level of vibration and consciousness than most humans possess. This sphere of being is the highest state of consciousness and the most sublime vibration, second only to the united harmony of the whole Tree. The Crown is both our origin and our destiny. We came from it and are destined to unite with it again. One may think of it as God-consciousness.

When the Great I AM conceived us, it put a bit of itself in each of us, the little "I am" of the Great I AM. This explains God's answer to Moses when he asked what name he should use with the people waiting for his return: "I am that I am." Our sense of "I am" is a reflection of the Supreme Being, the Great I AM, who conceived us and is always within us.

Notice that the first emanation on the Tree of Life has a direct connection with the tenth emanation, exactly as the Great I AM has with the little "I am." The crown also symbolizes rulership, and the Scriptures teach that we are heirs to the kingdom of our Father.

Hearken, my beloved brethren; did not God choose them that are poor as to the world to be rich in faith, and heirs of the kingdom which he promised to them that love him?" —James 2:5

As difficult as it may be to accept, we are sons and daughters of the Creator:

"God has taken his place in the divine council; in the midst of the gods he holds judgment. I said, 'You are gods, sons [and daughters] of the Most High, all of you.'" —Psalm 82:2, 6; RSV

How do we, who are so far from this awareness and level of being, reach our godly potential? From Cayce's readings we find that the crown is gained by bearing the cross of subduing our earthly, selfish tendencies. Consider these two Bible passages:

God created man in his own image. In God's image he created him; male and female he created them. God blessed them. God said to them, "Be fruitful, multiply, fill the earth, and subdue it." —Genesis 1:27-28, RSV;

God said to Cain, "Sin is crouching at the door [of your mind and heart]; its desire is for you, but you must master it." —Genesis 4:7, RSV;

Think about this. How could a three-dimensional, physical being, with a materialistic mind and a heart full of earthly desires, reach into the consciousness and presence of the Creator of the entire universe and all that is in it? It would require a significant transformation and transcendence. Fortunately, there is powerful help. Also, the transition is accomplished one step at a time—here a little, there a little—until the whole journey is complete and the crown is received.

The writers of Kabbalah consider this first state of consciousness to be "Concealed Consciousness."

Emanation 2 Wisdom

The God-consciousness of the first emanation naturally leads to the second emanation: Wisdom. Such wisdom comes not from knowledge, experience, or study but from receptiveness to God and God's responding blessing. The Scriptures have this to say:

Where shall wisdom be found? And where is the place of understanding? Man knoweth not the price thereof; neither is it found in the land of the living. The deep saith, "It is not in me"; and the sea saith, "It is not with me." It cannot be gotten for gold, neither shall silver be weighed for the price thereof. Whence then cometh wisdom? And where is the place of understanding? Seeing it is hid from the eyes of all living, and kept close from the birds of the heavens, Destruction and Death say, "We have heard a rumor thereof with our ears. God understands the way thereof, and he knows the place thereof." —Job 28: 12-28; American Standard Version, ASV

God knows the place where wisdom hides, and contact with God brings this wisdom. As we lift our minds up to God, expanding our consciousness into the infinite mind of God, we gain this wisdom. It is an inner knowing that comes to us as from out of nowhere, seemingly from everywhere. The more we lift ourselves into God-consciousness, the more we become godlike.

This wisdom is like intuition. It is humble, not self-exalting. It even surprises us at times because we know we did not conceive it; it simply came upon us, a natural consequence of our increasing proximity to God's all-knowing mind.

Surprisingly, throughout the Scriptures, a criterion for wisdom is "fear of the Lord." In this passage from the book of Job, we find this same idea expressed by God:

And unto man He [God] said, "Behold, the fear of the Lord, that is wisdom; and to depart from evil is understanding." —Job 28:28

Fear of the Lord may be understood as the fear to misapply knowledge we gain from our growing relationship with the All-Knowing. Imagine how disciplined we would have to be if we gained all-knowingness. If we knew the hearts and minds of everyone we met, we'd have to have control of our human tendency to judge, even condemn. If we gained precognitive knowing, imagine how tempted we would be to abuse this advantage. Thus, to avoid shattering the vessel of our own consciousness, the orb of our being must first hold to an alert concern for misapplication of the knowledge God's presence bestows upon us. This is the beginning of wisdom.

Returning to the emanation of Wisdom, a key to "receiving" (as the term Kabbalah means "to receive") the emanation of wisdom is selflessness. As the individual empties itself of its own interests, desires, and willfulness, it makes room for God to flow in.

The consciousness Kabbalists associate with this emanation is the Illuminating Consciousness. This consciousness generates action. It is a light that seeks to reach out. We have the creative plan in the Crown; now we have the impetus, the enlightened and inspired desire to bring forward the creation according to the plan. A. Action is a quality of wisdom.

Cayce agrees with this Kabbalistic view of wisdom, saying that for knowledge or understanding to become wisdom, it must be applied in life. Wisdom results from action. Wisdom is the creative plan in action. It is not a static state of being or knowing. God gives the gift and we apply it in life.

This emanation is considered to be masculine, and as such, it is known as the Father of Fathers. It is also considered to be Eden, in the sense that the Garden was the prototype, or pattern, for companionship with our Creator. In the midst of this Garden is the Water of Life. Writes of Kabbalah have called it the "Wisdom-Gushing Fountain," the "Water of the Wise," that bathes and nourishes those who enjoy the counsel of God, enabling them to share their lives and consciousness with their Creator's in communion through prayer, meditation, inner listening, and being conduits of God's love and grace to others.

Emanation 3 Understanding and Insight

The Crown of God-consciousness and the subsequent Wisdom that follow lead to the third emanation: Understanding. Here the individual soul's mind gains perception, comprehension, and appreciation.

These first three emanations are beautifully expressed in the following passages of Scripture:

"Get wisdom; get understanding. Forget it not; neither decline from the words of my mouth. Forsake her not, and she shall preserve thee. Love her, and she shall keep thee. Wisdom is the principal thing; therefore get wisdom. And with all thy getting get understanding. Exalt her, and she shall promote thee. She shall bring thee to honor, when thou dost embrace her. She shall give to your head an ornament of grace, a crown of glory shall she deliver to thee." —Proverbs 4:5-9, KJV

The concept of the interrelatedness of our relationship with God and our relationship with others is reminiscent of a biblical teaching about the greatest commandment:

"A lawyer asked him a question, to test him. 'Teacher, which is the great commandment in the law?' And he said to him, 'You shall love the Lord your God with all your heart, and with all your soul, and with all your mind. This is the great and first commandment. And a second is like it, you shall love your neighbor as yourself. On these two commandments depend all the law and the prophets.'" —Matthew 22:36-40; WEB

In this answer, Jesus is quoting from Deuteronomy 6:5 for the first commandment, and from Leviticus 19:18 for the second. But the point we need to catch here is that loving others is "like" loving God, as the second commandment is like the first. How can this be, when we may more easily develop a good relationship with God than we can with others? We may see others as so difficult to live with—so muddled, so willful, so diverse in their ways. The answer lies in a realization that the God we love, though very personal, is in fact infinite, and all beings exist within God; and God cares about them all. In fact, the piece of God placed in us is also in each of them—as imperfect as they (and we) may be. This is the understanding required of us, and in order to fulfill the second commandment, we must change our focus to minimize their weaknesses and vices, and maximize their strengths and virtues. This then reflects again upon us as a natural effect of the law of karma, of action and reaction. If we understand and minimize others' weaknesses and vices, our weaknesses and vices will be understood and minimized. The emanation of Understanding is considered to be female, and as such, it is the Mother of Mothers. The Mother (Understanding) blends with the Father (Wisdom) to produce the Logos, the central monad of all consciousness.

Here we come to a complexity of these teachings that we need to consider. The vast, infinite, unseen essence of God, interacting with the spirit of the emanated Father and Mother, created the Logos— what Kabbalah calls Adam Kadmon, meaning "Primal Being." This is very similar to the Hindu teaching of the Cosmic Beingness—*Purushad*—the original self-awareness that pervades the entire creation and is the state of God's being made knowable. The Logos allows our conscious communion with God.

The Primal Being, or the Logos, is not an intermediary keeping us from direct contact with our Creator, as some write, but a conduit from where we are to where God's pure, pre-Creation presence abides. The Logos is one with Concealed God; it is a comprehendible expression of Concealed God. Remember, the brilliance and awesome energy of the Infinite Eternal One had to retreat into the deep for the Creation to occur. Through the expression of Father (wisdom) and Mother (understanding), and their blending, we have an access to the Creator, whose presence will not destroy us; this is the Logos. The Logos is the Avatar of all avatars, the Collective Consciousness of all consciousnesses. It is the Messiah prophesied by the archangel Gabriel to the prophet Daniel. Each individual may unite its consciousness with this Universal Consciousness, and in its role as Messiah, it redeems and enlightens everyone who opens and receives it.

Jesus, filled with the Spirit of the Logos, explained it this way:

"In that day you will know that I am in my Father, and you in me, and I in you." —John 14:20

"In that day you will ask in my name; and I do not say to you that I shall pray the Father for you; for the Father himself loves you." —John 16: 26

Here are the first lines of John's Gospel:

"In the beginning was the Word (Logos),and the Logos was with God, and the Logos was God. This One was in the beginning with God; all things were made through this One, and without this One was not anything made that was made. In this One was life, and the life was the light of men. The light shines in the darkness, and the darkness has not overcome it." —John 1:1-5

Note: There is no masculine pronoun in the original text; the term is "this One," not "he," as in so many Bible translations of this passage.

As you can see from this passage, we are speaking about the Primal Being, its consciousness and its role.

It was the Primal Being (*Adam Kadmon*) who communed with God in the Garden of Eden. The Primal Being is the Father of Fathers, the Mother of Mothers, and all the children live within its Universal Consciousness. This means that a deep aspect of ourselves communed with God in the Garden.

This consciousness touches the pre-Creation God's Concealed Consciousness, and it is through this Logos that we come to know the Infinite Eternal One—albeit intuitively, in a manner that is a knowing unlike normal human knowing. More on this as we continue.

Writers of Kabbalah consider the consciousness of this emanation to be the "Sanctifying Mind." We can see how this fits well with the effect of the Messiah consciousness on our minds.

The triad of the first three emanations—I AM, the Father of Fathers, and the Mother of Mothers—creates the center essence of all consciousness, all life. From out of this triad, at the top of the Tree of Life, comes all the following emanations.

Kabbalah Study Guide – Van Auken

The Next Triad

Emanation 4 Loving Kindness and Mercy

Now we move into the heart (not the pump). Here we have the sphere of the fourth emanation: Loving Kindness and Mercy. If we are to know God, to companion with our Creator, then we must become loving and merciful, for these are attributes of God.

When God directed the building of that most mysterious device for communicating directly with Him—the Ark of the Covenant—one of the last features to be added was a mercy seat, protected by two angels. God instructed Moses:

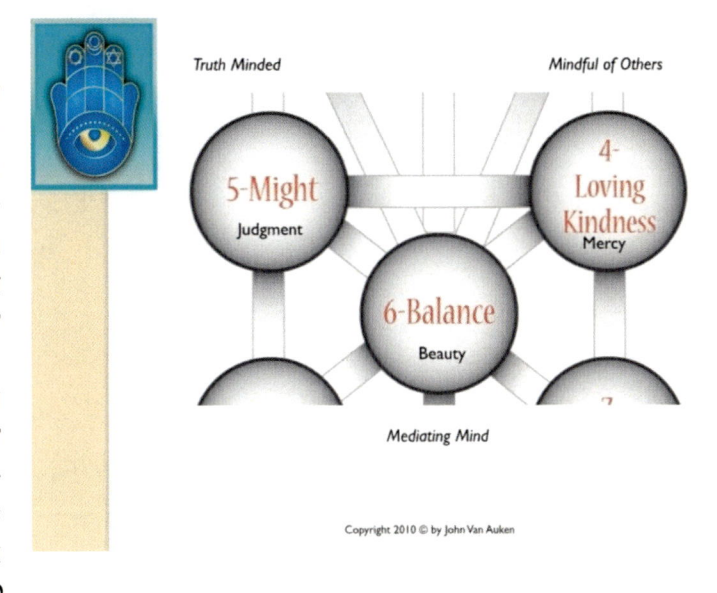

"You shall make a mercy seat of pure gold; two cubits and a half (45") shall be its length, and a cubit and a half (27") its breadth. And you shall make two cherubim of gold; of hammered work shall you make them, on the two ends of the mercy seat. Make one cherub on the one end, and one cherub on the other end; of one piece with the mercy seat shall you make the cherubim on its two ends. The cherubim shall spread out their wings above, overshadowing the mercy seat with their wings, their faces one to another; toward the mercy seat shall the faces of the cherubim be. And you shall put the mercy seat on the top of the ark [of the Covenant]; and in the ark you shall put the testimony that I shall give you. There I will meet with you, from above the mercy seat, from between the two cherubim that are upon the ark of the testimony...." –Exodus 25:17-22; RSV

Mercy is a required energy, consciousness, and disposition for direct communication with God. God seeks to commune with us and has arranged for us to make contact with that knowledge that He is all-merciful so that, even with our many weaknesses, we may come to Him.

Today this ark, its angels, and its mercy seat have moved into our hearts and minds. They are no longer external devices. It is here within us that the Divine wishes to meet and commune with us.

The disciple Paul wrote about this communion, using the model of the Ark of the Covenant and the Mercy Seat:

"The first covenant had regulations for worship and an earthly sanctuary. For a tent was prepared, the outer one, in which were the lamp stand [seven-candled menorah] and the table and the bread of the Presence; it is called the Holy Place. Behind the second curtain stood a tent called the Holy of Holies, having the golden altar of incense and the ark of the covenant covered on all sides with gold, which contained a golden urn holding the manna, and Aaron's rod that budded, and the tables of the covenant; above it were the cherubim of glory overshadowing the mercy seat. Of these things we cannot now speak in detail. ... When Christ [i.e., Adam Kadmon, Primal Being, the Word, the Logos] appeared as a high priest of the good things that have come, then through the greater and more perfect tent (not made with hands, that is, not of this creation) he entered once for all into the Holy Place, taking not the blood of goats and calves but his own blood, thus securing an eternal redemption. For if the sprinkling of defiled persons with the blood of goats and bulls and with the ashes of a heifer sanctifies for the purification of the flesh, how much more shall the blood of Christ [the Logos], who through the eternal Spirit offered himself without blemish to God, purify your conscience from dead works to serve the living God. Therefore he is the mediator of a new covenant, so that those who are called may receive the promised eternal inheritance.... Christ [the Logos] has entered, not into a sanctuary made with hands, a copy of the true one, but into heaven itself, now to appear in the presence of God on our behalf." —Hebrews 9:1-24; RSV

Writers of Kabbalah consider the consciousness of this emanation to be "Mindful of Others," quite naturally a condition of mercy and lovingkindness.

Emanation 5 Judgment and Might

Here's a paradox: how can the disposition of lovingkindness and mercy naturally flow into the fifth emanation of Might and Judgment? If real power is love and good judgment is mercy, what is the role of this fifth emanation?

The secret is that might and power, as it emanates from God, is more the nature of faith and patience. This is the secret of the mystical quality of longsuffering, that so misunderstood by many. Why is long-suffering a virtue and listed among the various fruits of the Spirit? First, it is a quality of God:"But thou, O Lord, art a God full of compassion, and gracious, longsuffering, and plenteous in mercy and truth." (Psalm 86:15/16 depending upon which translation you're readying.) "The Lord passed by before him [Moses] and proclaimed, 'The Lord, The Lord God, [is] merciful and gracious, longsuffering, and abundant in goodness and truth.'" (Exodus 34:6) And second, the path that a human must walk in an attempt to awaken to his or her godly nature and godly role with the Creator requires many profound changes in the heart and mind, changes that bring painful adjustments. One must live through these with faith, patience, and longsuffering in order to reach the goal. This is the might of the fifth emanation.

This human-to-godling journey of the soul has been compared to a woman pregnant, in this respect: we have conceived in the womb of our consciousness that our truer nature is godly, or divine; we have gestated this to full term; now the process requires that we dilate our hearts and minds to deliver this eternal part of ourselves! It is as painful an adjustment as a woman's birth canal dilating to deliver a new baby. There are many cycles of labor pains and various stages in the process of birth, as there are in the journey of our spiritual birth. Much suffering occurs as the earthly desires, habits, and beliefs are moved out of the way for the passage of the divine self and its perspectives. The shift from self-driven will to cooperative will with God's will is challenging. It is a breakthrough physically, mentally, emotionally, and spiritually. Anyone who has been on the so-called spiritual path for any length of time knows this.

Kabbalists consider the consciousness of this emanation to be "Truth Minded." In this we again have the paradoxical balancing of Love with Truth. Might and judgment are not blind to truth while maintaining love and mercy. Many call this "tough love." It is a love that does not ignore the truth of the situation, the relationship, or the pattern of actions and thoughts yet maintains a loving, merciful manner. These contending forces lead us to the next emanation.

Kabbalah Study Guide – Van Auken
Emanation 6 Beauty and Balance

We have seen how lovingkindness and mercy lead to an unusual form of might and judgment, and these now lead to the sixth emanation: Beauty and Balance.

The quality of beauty in this emanation was well stated by the poet John Keats (1795-1821) in his Ode on a Grecian Urn: "Beauty is truth, truth beauty—that is all ye know on earth, and all ye need to know." The Truth Mindedness of the previous emanation naturally leads to Beauty and Balance.

In Proverbs 20:29, "The beauty of old men is the grey head," and, in Proverbs 16:31, the grey head is a "crown of glory." In plain words, God finds beauty in one's having lived rightly and gaining the truth that is found in old age.

The greater balance comes when truth is balanced with love. To achieve balance, one must maintain the presence of truth.

In this respect, we must balance our personal needs and duty to God with our role as channels of God's love and light to others—our inner nourishment and our outer service must find a balance. When there is imbalance, Cayce warned, the physical (the flesh) will win out, for it is the weaker part of us.

This leads to another consideration related to our paradoxical nature of being both human and divine. To retain sanity, we have to balance our physical and our spiritual development. Given this challenge, balance is one of the most important orbs on the Tree of Life.

In many respects, incarnate life is a balance of opposites. It requires amazing tranquility, the patience of Job, and the mindfulness of a tightrope walker. Kabbalists consider this emanation's consciousness to be the "Mediating Mind." One who strives for the beauty of truth and balance will be victorious, which leads us to the next emanation.

The Next Triad

Emanation 7 Victory and Fortitude

When the mind and the heart are enlivened by the first six emanations, the seventh naturally emerges: Victory and Fortitude. This emanation and the next two are said to depict God's activity in manifested life on earth.

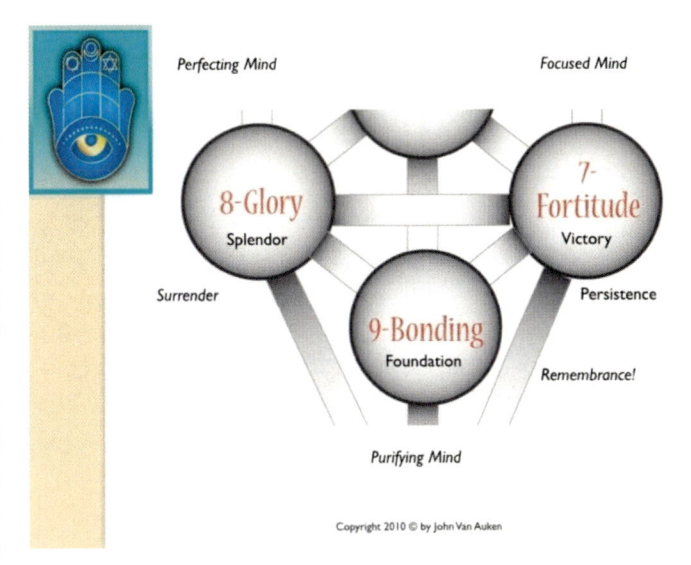

The seventh orb expresses the Divine's eternal quality of being. If one is eternal, then one innately has the fortitude to endure through all the challenges of animated life and will realize victory. The saying "this too shall pass" is a reminder that we should not get so upset about situations that appear to block or detour us from our ideal life, relationships, and health, because challenges will not endure and will not last forever. Yet God and our godly nature are eternal—forever. Therefore, good ultimately overcomes evil; hardship ultimately yields to harmony, joy, and contentment. This is our destiny; it ends in victory. As the Jewish teacher Jesus taught, "He who endures unto the end shall be saved." (Matthew 10:22; RSV) The very vibration of fortitude, endurance, and keeping on, generates a disposition that reflects that eternal, immortal portion of God's nature that is in each of us.

Considering our ultimate destiny as godlings within the Most High God, the disciple Paul wrote:
"Behold, I tell you a mystery: We all shall not sleep, but we shall all be changed, in a moment, in the twinkling of an eye, at the last trump; for the trumpet shall sound, and the dead shall be raised incorruptible, and we shall be changed. For this corruptible must put on incorruption, and this mortal must put on immortality. But when this corruptible shall have put on incorruption, and this mortal shall have put on immortality, then shall come to pass the saying that is written, 'Death is swallowed up in victory' [Isaiah 25:8]." —1 Corinthians 15:51-54

We all will eventually put on immortality. It is our deeper nature. We all will eventually be raised up to perfection and put on incorruption—forever. Holding this in our hearts and minds as we walk this strange journey will ensure our victory over all that besets us—whether it be within us or around us or both. There is an ember of immortality and perfection within us. And though it is a mystery today, we will all be changed in the twinkling of an eye, as the Scripture states, and our eternal, divine self will emerge. Fortitude is required now. Victory will be ours.

The Kabbalists consider this consciousness to be "Focused Mind," and rightly so, for such a journey as ours requires just that.

Emanation 8 Splendor and Glory

The realization of the earlier emanations brings us more in harmony and compatibility with our Creator's nature, allowing us to draw even closer. Such proximity to the Divine expresses the eighth emanation: Splendor and Glory. With this vibration and awareness, one is filled with light and patient peace. Why worry when God is so near? This is the presence of the Divine with us on our journey—and much easier is our journey with God's companionship.

Let's consider what this may be like in both the macrocosm and our microcosm. We begin with Scripture's description of the descent of God upon Mt. Sinai to bring the new Temple, the Ten Commandments, the Ark of the Covenant, and most importantly, His very Presence into the physical world. The Lord said to Moses, "Come up to me on the mountain, and wait there; and I will give you the tables of stone, with the law and the commandment, which I have written for their instruction." So Moses rose with his servant Joshua, and Moses went up into the mountain of God. And he said to the elders, "Tarry here for us, until we come to you again; and, behold, Aaron and Hur are with you; whoever has a cause, let him go to them." Then Moses went up on the mountain, and the cloud covered the mountain. The glory of the Lord settled on Mount Sinai, and the cloud covered it six days; and on the seventh day he called to Moses out of the midst of the cloud. Now the appearance of the glory of the Lord was like a devouring fire on the top of the mountain in the sight of the people of Israel. And Moses entered the cloud, and went up on the mountain. And Moses was on the mountain forty days and forty nights. —Exodus 24:12-18

This biblical passage is a key to understanding this emanation: It appears that the Infinite and we little, finite, heartfelt seekers cannot meet—as indicated in Job: "And now men cannot look on the light when it is bright in the skies, when the wind has passed and cleared them [clouds]. Out of the north comes golden splendor; God is clothed with terrible majesty." (Job 37:21-22) Who can look upon the

Omnipotent? Ah, but we underestimate the Omnipotent's love for us. God cloaked His terrifying majesty in a form that allows us to approach, as did Moses and Joshua.

There is a correlation between the macrocosmic Mount and the microcosmic crown chakra of the human body, located at the top of the head, the newborn's soft spot. This idea is also found in Hopi legend, in which "Great Uncle" guided his people to the new world by communicating to them via the soft spot on top of their heads. The crown chakra is the sacred mount in us. If we raise our energy and consciousness to this area wait quietly upon the Spirit, as God instructed Moses to do, guidance will come to us. "Be still, and know that I am God." (Psalm 46:10)

The splendor and glory of the Lord may be known. The Omnipotent will respond to our desire to commune. A cleansing, a preparation, and a transition may be required, but God so loves us that a way may be prepared for us to unite. We have to do our part: seek and prepare ourselves to be in the presence of the Almighty. One element of this preparation is implied in the Hebrew word for this emanation: Hod. It has a connotation of "submission." By subduing our will to God's will, God may descend upon the "mount" of our consciousness in a form that will not kill us or do irreparable harm. This begins the covenant between us and our Creator, and continues as an eternal relationship. The Splendor and Glory may be ours to experience and enjoy.

According to the Kabbalists, the consciousness associated with this emanation is "Perfecting Mind." Sharing our consciousness with God leads to the perfecting of our minds.

Emanation 9 Foundation and Bonding

Experiencing the glory and splendor of the Presence of God builds Foundation and Bonding: the ninth emanation. From this place, this condition, all things take on a new order, and goodness abides with us. As the biblical injunction states this truth, "Seek ye first the kingdom of God, and His righteousness; and all these things shall be added unto you." (Matthew 6:33; KJV) With this established, a foundation has been laid and a bonding with the Divine has begun.

Some of qualities of the qualities of Foundation may be found in the Psalms and Proverbs:

"Righteousness and justice are the foundation of thy throne. Loving kindness and truth go before thy face. Blessed is the people that know the joyful sound. They walk, O Lord, in the light of thy countenance." —Psalms 89:14-15

"Righteousness and justice are the foundation of his throne." —Psalm 97:2

"When the whirlwind passes, the wicked is no more; but the righteous is an everlasting foundation." —Proverbs 10:25

In the Toledano Kabbalah teachings (Toledo, Spain, ca. 900s to 1300s), this orb is also associated with remembering. In the Old Testament book of Malachi, we have this little insight:

"Then they that feared the Lord spoke often one to another: and the Lord listened, and heard it, and a Book of Remembrance was written before Him for them that feared the Lord, and that thought on His name. And they shall be mine, said the Lord of hosts, in that day when I act they will be my precious possessions; and I will spare them, as a man spares his own son that serves him. Then shall you return, and discern between the righteous and the wicked, between him that serves God and him that serves him not." —Malachi 3:16-18

The Revelation speaks of the "Book of Life from the foundation of the world," in which are written the names of the souls who have earned a passport to heavenly realms. (Rev. 13:8 and 17:8) In the Psalms, we find:

"You keep track of my wanderings. You put my tears in your flask, in your record." —Psalm 56:8-9

"I come in the volume of the book that is written of me." —Psalm 40:7

"Thy eyes beheld my unformed substance; in thy book were written, every one of them, the days that were formed for me, when as yet there was none of them. How precious to me are Thy thoughts, O God! How vast is the sum of them! If I would count them, they are more than the sand. When I awake, I am still with Thee." —Psalm 139:17-19

The true foundation lies with the Spirit of God, the Spirit of Life that is Eternal Life. The ideal must ever be founded upon something that is continuous; and only the Spirit is continuous!

This emanation is also associated with "bonding," a bonding that comes from sharing one's life with God, by inviting God into one's life and one's relationships and living the life together. It also requires our seeking to know God's presence and God's will and allowing God to share these with us. This builds the bond in our hearts and minds. This occurs not only through prayer but by inner listening to that still, small voice that Elijah heard in the cave and knew it to be the true voice of God, the voice that he could not find in the lightning, thunder, earthquake, or fire. (1 Kings 19:12) It was *within* him. It was still. How does one hear a still voice? One feels it. This is the mystical experience that builds the bond: prayer and deep, inner listening—not with our carnal ears but with the ear of our souls. Further, it comes more as a feeling of the Presence of God and God's guidance than the hearing of a voice. Elijah expressed it well: "a still, small voice within"—one feels a still voice.

Upon these aspects of the ninth emanation, we build an enduring foundation and bond with our Father-Mother Creator and eternal Companion.

Kabbalists identify the consciousness associated with this emanation as the "Purifying Mind."

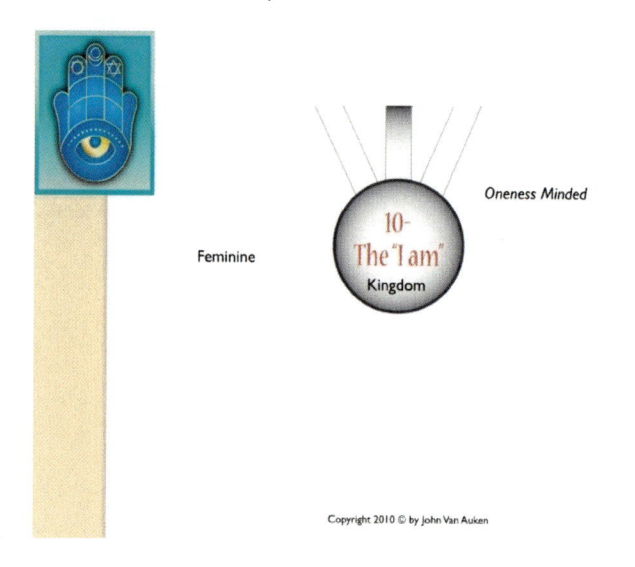

Emanation 10 Kingdom

This is the vessel (*kli*, in Hebrew; singular of *keilim*) that received the original burst of God's power and light at the moment of the big bang of Creation and did not break! When all other orbs shattered, this amazing little orb absorbed the Light of God and allowed it to flow back, repairing each of the broken orbs, until all was as it was intended to be. Out of the chaos came the repair that established the Kingdom of God and the Tree of Life.

Here is the true Holy of Holies, the zone where God has promised to meet us face to face. And though it is strange to us in our three-dimensional, projected life, this Kingdom is within us. Our being, the little "I am," is the temple of the living God, the Great I AM. And in this temple does the communion occur.

The disciple Paul, asked:

"Don't you know that you are a temple of God, and that the Spirit of God dwells in you?" and "Don't you know that your body is a temple of the Holy Spirit which is in you, which you have from God?" (1 Corinthians 6:19)

The disciple John alludes to this when he recounts in his gospel an event in which Jesus was asked, in the great temple in Jerusalem, to show the people a sign:

Jesus answered them, "Destroy this temple, and in three days I will raise it up." The people at the temple said, "Forty-six years was this temple in building, and will you raise it up in three days?" But he spoke of the temple of his body." —John 2:19, RSV;

This orb, or emanation, is also known as *Shekhinah*, meaning the Divine Presence, and is the feminine aspect of God. In the womb of our consciousness we have conceived our godling nature and destiny. Here, in the tenth emanation, the "I am" is born anew and seeks to unite with the Great I AM of the first emanation, after which oneness, harmony, contentment, and life reign forever.

Adam's Secret Sin and the 10th Emanation

In the *Zohar*, the secret sin was that "Adam drove out et!" What is et? It is found in this little passage: "Yahweh Elohim expelled him from the Garden of Eden ... He drove out *et* Adam." (Genesis 3:23-24) Actually, there is no interpretation for the Hebrew term *et* because it is not really a word; it is simply an accusative particle of the sentence with Adam as the determinate objective. It does not have a meaning, simply a role in grammar. However, its odd placement in this passage caused Kabbalists, who studied these passages *ad infinitum*, to suspect that there was a *secret* message here. They came to believe that et was a code term related to the tenth emanation of God. (Here aspects of the story of Lilith and Eve get involved, but it can become so complicated as to be of little use to us, so I am deferring this to the angels section of this course and a better context in which to address it.)

Now stay with me for a few more details before we actually know what "et" is.

Kabbalists believed that the *Shekhinah* (meaning "The dwelling place of the Divine Presence") is symbolized by the Tree of the Knowledge of Good and Evil that was in the Garden of Eden. Adam's sin was that he worshiped and partook of "Her" alone [the lower physical expression of the Divine expressed in the knowledge of good and evil], not in harmony with the other nine emanations. This split "Her" (the Feminine Divine) off from the Tree of Life and "divorced" Her from Her "husband," *Tiferet* (Beauty, Glory), the sixth emanation of Balance. Now there became an imbalance in the Cosmos. This disrupted the unity of the Cosmos and the harmony and balance that God had initially established.

Here is the passage from the *Zohar*. Rabbi El'azar said:

"We do not know who divorced whom, if the Blessed Holy One divorced Adam or not. But the word is transposed: 'He drove out et.' Et, precisely! And who drove out Et? Adam. Adam drove out Et! Therefore it is written: 'YHWH Elohim expelled him from the Garden of Eden.' Why did He expel him? Because Adam drove out Et, as we have said."

Traditionally, Adam's principal sin was believed to have been disobedience - eating the forbidden fruit of the Tree of the Knowledge of Good and Evil. However, his secret sin was knowing right from wrong. This knowledge caused Adam to hide from God for he now knew that his actions and desires were out of harmony with God's.

In the Bible, the expulsion from the Garden comes right after this passage spoken by Yahweh Elohim: "Behold, the man has become like one of us, knowing good and evil; and now, lest he put forth his hand and take also of the tree of life, and eat, and live forever..."—here the passage abruptly shifts to the expulsion from the Garden! Why? Souls were never meant to live in terrestrial physicality forever, but were in the image and likeness of their Creator, so they were destined to be celestial, heavenly beings forever. Incarnation was temporary. It was an opportunity to make choices between right and wrong, and to being God's love and light into this temporary world and the experiences of other souls.

For the Kabbalists, the secret sin was that Adam so desired the feminine presence of God ("Her") as it was now expressed in physical matter in the form of woman, that he wanted to possess her for his own. This strange idea is reinforced in Genesis 6:2: "The sons of God saw the daughters of men that they were fair; and they took for wives all of them that they chose." The creation of physical woman brought the Divine Presence into physical manifestation, and the sons of God broke from their spiritual "marriage" to heavenly Feminine God ("Her") and they turned all their attention and consciousness toward physically expressed Feminine. And this was not just to appreciate the pleasing beauty and pleasant demeanor of the Divine Feminine in physical form, no. If they had then it presumed all would be okay. But "sons" became driven by desire and craving for the Feminine, and to take possession of Her for their own gratification and glory.

Now believe me when I tell you that I too thought this might just the fears of old rabbis with their private lusts for women. But as I searched and researched various scholarly sources on biblical words and names, I became convinced that the powerful drive of males for females (sometimes without concern for their feelings and well being) was a metaphysical consequence of separating the original nature of our soul's yin and yang in oneness of spirit and mind. When these were divided into two separate expressions in two separate bodies (female and male), then an imbalance occurred. Kabbalists saw this as "divorcing" the spiritual for possession of the physical. Woman, from a metaphysical perspective, is the archetypal expression of the Divine Feminine in human form. And as such, she is exactly as the Scriptures first called her, "chavvah," meaning in Hebrew "life giver." In Genesis 3:20 Adam turns to his woman (isha in Hebrew, ish is man or male) and names her "life, life giver" (chavvah) not Eve as we have it (though Evah would also imply "life"). And he then explains this by saying, "for she is mother of all," which correlates her to the Divine Mother and the "Womb of God."

The separation of the Divine Feminine into an individualized, physical expression was so appealing that the spiritual godlings ("sons of God") that they "divorced" their marriage to the Spirit and sought only the physical bonding with the physical Shekhinah, meaning the majestic presence of God in physical expression as woman. This drove Adam to carry her away from her marriage to the heavenly Tree of Life. But this could not be allowed to go on forever, so God brought the cycle of death and rebirth upon them until this could be resolved—keeping them from making this a permanent condition. And that was done by guarding their access to the Tree of Life, indicating immortality. Interestingly, in the last chapters of the book of Revelation, the redemption of this situation is realized: the Bride is presented to the heavenly Groom, and the sons and daughters of God are again allowed to eat from the Tree of Life and live forever. (Rev. 20-22) Interestingly, Jesus uses this metaphor too in his parable of the Bribe, the Bribegroom, and the ten virgins with their oil lamps in Matthew 25. Ten emanations, ten virgins, bride, and bridegroom?? Sounds like the Kabbalah Tree of Life and the secret story of Adam and Eve (Chavvah). Hmm, was Jesus trained in the Kabbalah?

Keep in mind that what I've just shared is an archetypal dynamic, not an individual one. Each individual woman is an individual with her own dynamics and soul-karma patterns. But woman as a whole is the expression of the Divine Life Giver. Also, in this metaphor Adam does NOT represent individual men. Adam or man as a whole represents the power and strength to do good or evil with the Life Giver as expressed in physicality. And he, as an archetype and we as individuals, must learn to master this power, just as God taught Cain, the wayward son of Adam: "Sin lies at the door (of your consciousness) and its desire is for you. You must master it." Furthermore, each individual woman and man has both of these dynamics within them, yin and yang, and they are wrestling for resolution and balance. Women must get in touch with their inner masculine or animus, and men with their inner feminine, or anima, if each is to gain their whole consciousness.

The tenth emanation is the home of the awakening of the little "I am" and its relationship with the Great I AM. The divorce must be healed and a new marriage occur, a marriage of the individual to the Universal, of the finite to the Infinite, of the physical to the Spiritual. It is the place of meeting the Divine Presence. And that place is in the bodily temple of the individual heart, mind, and soul, communing with the Universal Mind and Infinite Spirit. Separation is not an eternal option; union and oneness are the ultimate conditions for true happiness and eternal life. And "as within so without." Out here in this life we must grasp the higher qualities of woman and man, and their mutual relationship with the Divine Presence in Spirit and Mind.

Kabbalists consider this emanation's consciousness to be the "Oneness Mind," expressing the need to stop the separation and reunite in oneness.

Let's recap the ten emanations:

1. The "I AM," Crown, Concealed Consciousness
2. Wisdom, Illuminating Mind
3. Understanding, Sanctifying Mind
4. Mercy and Loving Kindness, Mindful of Others
5. Judgment and Might, Truth Minded
6. Balance and Beauty, Mediating Mind
7. Victory and Fortitude, Focused Mind
8. Splendor and Glory, Perfecting Mind
9. Foundation and Bonding, Purifying Mind
10. The "I am," Kingdom, Oneness Minded.

Da'at — Knowledge

Some schools of Kabbalah add an emanation called Knowledge, or Da'at, in Hebrew, often written Daat. There are various interpretations surrounding this sphere. The location of the sefirah Da'at in the so-called "empty place" in the Tree, but this empty place is classically considered to be the Abyss or "the deep," which is in the second sentence of the Bible: "darkness was upon the face of the deep." (Genesis 1:2) The Deep is a very special place in the Tree of Life. I believe it to be the "portal" to Infinity.

The Abyss — "The Deep"

Notice the "Abyss" in the classic layout of the Tree of the Life, considered to be the Empty Place, the Deep, or the Void of Eastern teachings. This empty space is believed to be a portal, an opening from the visible universe to the invisible. Did you know the entire universe that we see is only 4 percent of the whole universe? Yes, 96 percent of the universe is invisible, yet we know its there by the effects it has on the visible. As such, the Deep is a mystically significant region in the Tree of Life. Blocking this passageway—especially with something as cluttering as knowledge (Da'at)—does not seem wise. Therefore, some schools omit Da'at, feeling that is a misunderstanding by some teachers. The stillness, quiet, and silence that abides in this empty space are the qualities required to pass through this portal to the Infinite Eternal One. "Be still, and know that I am God." (Psalm 46:10)

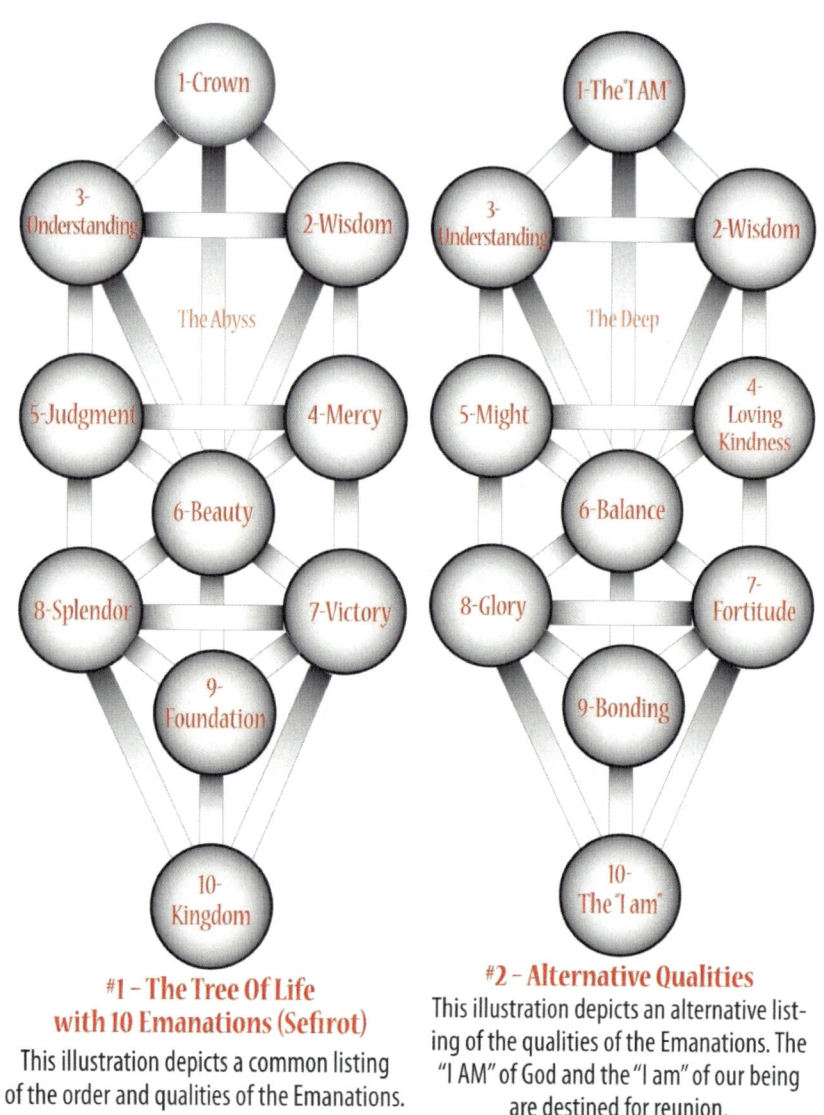

#1 – The Tree Of Life with 10 Emanations (Sefirot)
This illustration depicts a common listing of the order and qualities of the Emanations.

#2 – Alternative Qualities
This illustration depicts an alternative listing of the qualities of the Emanations. The "I AM" of God and the "I am" of our being are destined for reunion.

To clarify, this abyss is not the pit into which Satan is cast. It is not the pit of evil darkness. It is the fathomless "deep" of God's mind and being. It is the womb of pre-creation. In here is a stillness, a silence, that rejuvenates and rebirths our soul. It is the original home, with which our souls long to

30

reconnect. The primal sacred sound OM reminds us of this place of our origin, of our heavenly "hOMe."

When we view the Tree of Life's structure, we see three pillars.

There are Three Pillars

The 10 emanations are also divided into two sets of the three pillars. One set is the pillars of the feminine (yin), masculine (yang), and the blend. The other set is the pillar of severity, mercy, and mildness.

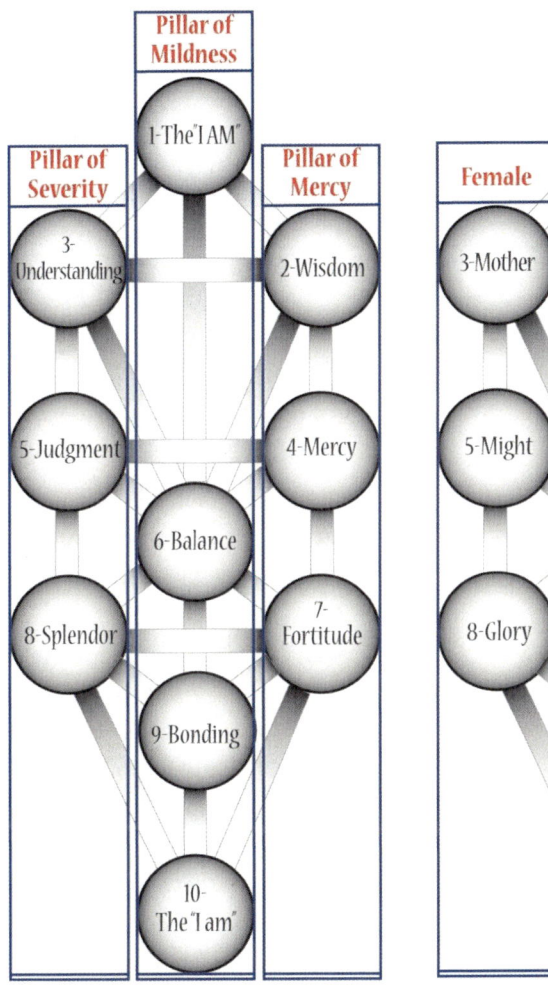

#10 – The 3 Pillars
This illustration depicts the three pillars:
Severity, Mildness, and Mercy.

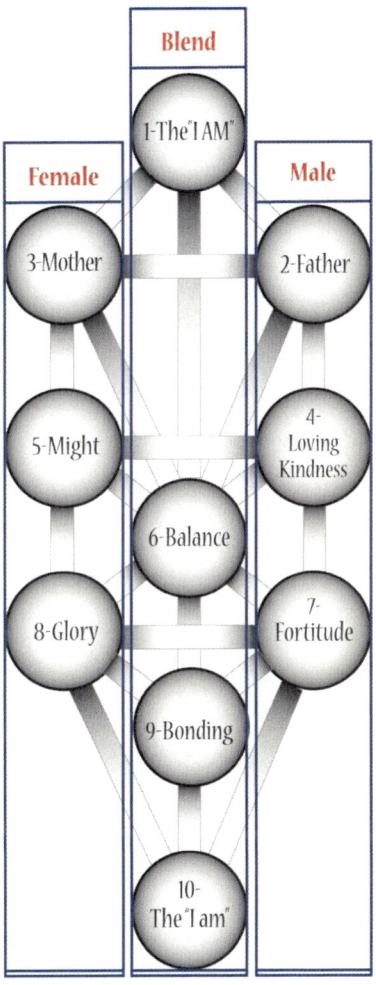

#11 – The 3 Pillars
This illustration depicts the three pillars:
Female, Blend, and Male.

Kabbalah Study Guide – Van Auken

There are also 22 channels:

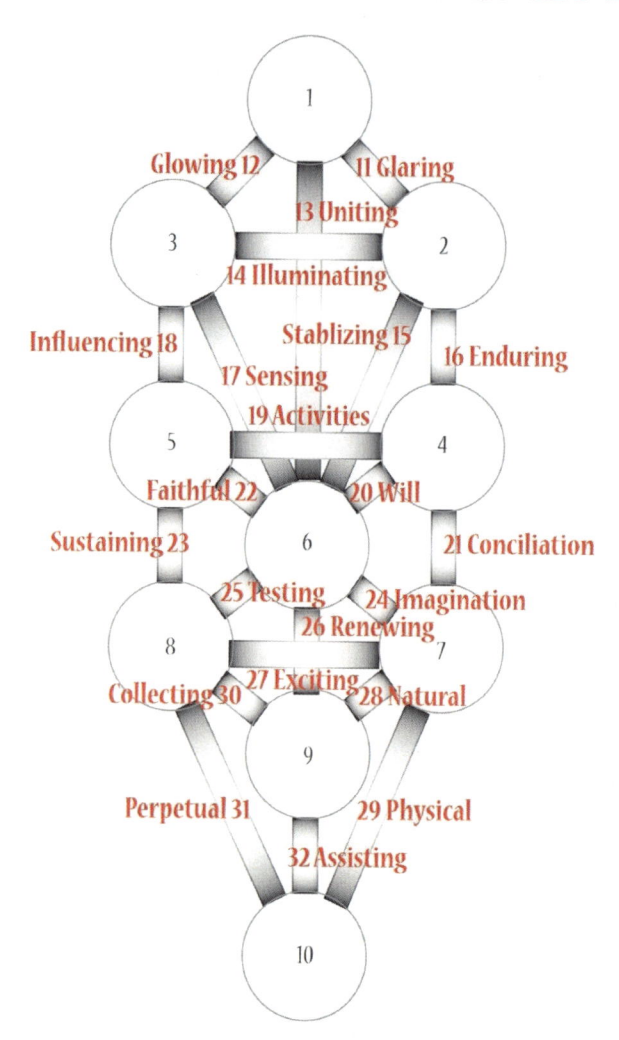

#7 - The 22 Pathways/Channels
This illustration depicts the 22 pathways or channels that run between the orbs. They number from 11 to 32.

Again, please don't let yourself get lost in this complexity. Just read it as a curious facet of Kabbalah lore, remembering that your deeper mind sees through the same eyes that you do, and it will grasp what is needed for your soul growth.

The "22" Pathways The Life Forces Flow Through Us and We through Them

The Twenty-Two Mystical Pathways (*Nativot Phayliot*) are a network that circulates qualities of consciousness and energy throughout the Tree of Life. Because each of the twenty-two pathways runs between two specific emanations, respectively, they are each unique. For example, the pathway that runs between the Great I AM and Beauty is naturally going to be different from the one that runs between the little "I am" and Bonding—with respect to the qualities of both consciousness and energy. (NOTE: 22 is the total number because the 10 emanational orbs precede the actual conduits, paths, or channels. Therefore there are actually 32 paths or channels: 10 plus 22.)

The pathways are ethereal, but they do reach into the physical universe and, most importantly, into our hearts, minds, and even our physical bodies. In this they are both macrocosmic and microcosmic forces. In this study, we are going to focus more on the personal, microcosmic influences that affect our soul life.

Each of these twenty-two pathways corresponds to one of the twenty-two letters of the Hebrew alphabet, and each of the pathways has a number associated with it that reflects its order in the sequence of the Tree of Life. Since the Tree has 10 emanations, the first pathway number is 11. And since, in this time frame, we are already deep in the Creation, and much of what we are doing is flowing back through the Tree of Life (at least it feels that way to us), we will begin our study with the pathway that is closest to our present state of being, number 32, and proceed from there to the highest, 11.

Much of the detail about this network comes from Kabbalah's The Book of Creation (Sefer Yetzirah) and subsequent writings and interpretations, such as The Tree of Life (Kuntres Etz HaChayim), a Chassidic treatise circa 1700s, by Rabbi Shalom DovBer Schneersohn of Lubavitch.

There is a tendency to develop a linear view of these pathways, but they are interconnected, just as the emanations are. We can and do experience all of them, even when we are mostly focusing on just one. Let's try to keep a holistic view as we read these in order, beginning with the little "I am" and moving up to the Great I AM.

The Pathways/Channels

32 – The Assisting Path

As we begin, the Creation is already in full swing. Now we are returning through the ten emanations and twenty-two pathways. Thus we begin with pathway 32. How did I get the number 32? The 10 orbs are numbered first and then we add the 22 channels, giving us 32 elements in the Tree of Life. This channel connects the tenth emanation of our "I Am" and the Kingdom with the ninth emanation: Foundation. The awareness that runs along this pathway is called "Worshipped Consciousness" (Sekhel Ne'evad) as well as the "Assisting" or "Administrative" Consciousness and Energy. These terms relate to phases of our development. As we first awaken to spiritual awareness and higher vibrations, we worship this enlightenment and energy as a gift from God. They are a hidden well of renewing water in the very dry desert of materiality and self-conscious life. As its flow increases and we become more receptive vessels, our consciousness and energy become more comfortable and familiar with this pathway, so it moves from a worshiping to an assisting influence in the spiritualization of our bodies and minds. This pathway is also known as a destroyer. As such, our earthly self may become scared, wanting to hide from the terrifying power of God's growing proximity. But this destroyer is as Hinduism's Shiva, a destroyer of illusions and a cleanser of the "unheavenly." In its role, this pathway destroys many of the idols we have developed and hold onto so tightly—such as passionate, earthly desires and self-gratifying habits. Of course, our earthly, egocentric self feels that it cannot live without these comforts and idols. But our soul senses the need to let go of them for the higher, more eternal good. This requires that we die a little to our earthliness to make room for heavenliness—just as our loving Creator died a little to Its perfection to allow us to make mistakes by virtue of our free will and to grow to understand that such a gift is a double-edged sword and must therefore be wielded with care.

31 – The Perpetual Path

Once we have been assisted in our first turn toward the Light and the vessels of our mind and body contain sufficient awareness and energy, we open the flow to and from the eighth emanation—Splendor and Glory—with that sweet quality of Surrender. This pathway is called "Continuous Consciousness" or "Perpetual Consciousness" (*Sekhel Tamidi*), so named because, once opened, it will never be closed; we will never fall back from this level of awareness and energy. Even if we fall away from spiritual seeking, we never forget having touched this level of awareness and energy.

All we have to do to open this pathway, no matter how earthly or even evil we have become, is to turn around from the darkness to face the Light. When we do so, all of our shadows fall behind and the path opens brightly before us. Nothing stands between us and our Creator but ourselves and our free will to step away. This pathway is associated with the two great lights in the sky: the sun and the moon, which represent, respectively, the Great I AM of the first emanation and the little "I am" of the tenth emanation. Though we live now in the moonlight of our little being, our destiny is to live in the sunlight of God's companionship.

30 – The Collecting Path

Now that we have Assistance (32) and have opened Perpetual Consciousness (31), we may flow through the "Collecting" or "Collective" Consciousness (*Sekhel Kelali*), sometimes called General Consciousness, in the sense of universal. It contains the *Ophanim*—celestial beings described in The Book of Enoch with the cherubim and seraphim as "never sleeping" but watching (or guarding) the throne of God. *Ophan* also means "wheels," as seen in Ezekiel's vision and Hinduism's chakras. This pathway is a vortex of celestial energy and awareness. This channel raises our vibrations and consciousness to a new and stronger level. It flows to and from the pools of Splendor and Foundation, bathing us in renewing light and gathering heavenly help to us.

29 – The Spirit-Filled Physical Path

Now victorious, we enjoy the vigor of the seventh emanation: Fortitude. This channel is called "Physical Consciousness" (*Sekhel Mugsham*), in the sense of giving life and growth to all of physical life. The essence of spirit invigorates form; spirit enlivens flesh and matter. Now our physical lives have a new level of energy and awareness that we have not enjoyed for a very long time, long before this incarnation.

28 – The Natural Path

This new vigor opens the flow to and from the ninth and seventh emanations through the pathway called "Natural Consciousness" (*Sekhel Mutba*), in the sense of Nature's life-giving ways and laws. Finally, we are in sync with the forces of Nature.

27 – The Exciting Path

Next is the "Exciting" or "Palpable Consciousness" (*Sekhel Murgash*). It is so named because the consciousness of all living things created under the entire upper realms were given life through this flowing pathway. Here is the élan vital, the metaphysical kundalini energy. Amazingly, the age that follows the end of the Mayan Age of Movement, ending on the winter solstice of December 21, 2012, is the Age of the Spirit of All Living Things—the age for this pathway. This pathway's consciousness and energy are the animators of manifested life, making all creators palpable, excited by the flow of life within them.

26 – The Renewing Pathway

Now we reach the energy of Renewing Consciousness (*Sekhel MeChudash*). Here all things are made new. Forgotten truths are renewed. Lost treasures of the soul are rediscovered. Here we feel our old selves again, as celestial souls rather than terrestrial bodies. Our spiritual being has been in suspension, lingering in a stasis since our entry into physical matter. Now our spirit stretches its wings again and awakens to live renewed.

25 – The Testing Pathway

The next channel is "Testing Consciousness" (*Sekhel Nisyoni*). Here is where we meet the "original temptation" to see if it still holds sway over us. This is where the Light Forces test all returning, renewed, and resurrected souls. On the descent it was a test we failed. On the ascent, it will be an easy one to pass, since we have come to know how much we lost and we are wiser from our experiences.

According to the Bible, this test is as by fire, in the sense that fire refines, or perfects, metals rather than destroys them:

"I will put this third [the renewed souls] into the fire, and refine them as one refines silver, and test them as gold is tested. They will call on my name, and I will answer them. I will say, 'They are my people'; and they will say, 'The Lord is my God.'" Zechariah 13:8-9

The disciple Paul picks up on this, writing: "Each man's work will become manifest; for the Day will disclose it, because it will be revealed with fire, and the fire will test what sort of work each one has done." I Corinthians 3:13

And, as Paul also wrote: God is a consuming fire, purging and cleansing those He loves, that they may be more perfect. Metals are made more perfect thought the testing by fire. Here we are speaking of the metaphysical fire of the Spirit, not the flames of combustion, as expressed by John the Baptist:

"I baptize you with water for repentance, but he who is coming after me is mightier than I, whose sandals I am not worthy to carry; he will baptize you with the Holy Spirit and with fire." –Matthew 3:11

24 – The Pathway of the Imagination

Now we have the flow of the "Imaginative" or "Apparitional Consciousness" (*Sekhel Dimyoni*), often called Apparitive Consciousness. This is the appearance of nonmaterial vessels, as apparitions. As strange as it seems to us living in three-dimensional matter, the imaginative forces are the pathway to higher consciousness and perception. Here we think of imagination as unreal fantasy, but thoughts are things in the realms of heaven and the Universal Consciousness. Our individualness is evident in this world by a separate physical body, but in the heavens, we have only our mind and soul, which have the qualities of apparitions, ghosts, and spirits, and in this realm the imaginative forces are real. Consider how free and expansive our mind would be beyond three dimensions, in a vast openness of infinity. This is the imaginative pathway. Nothing is beyond the mind's imagination. We could expand into infinity and no one could discern us from the Infinite, and in a flash, we could contract again, expressing our individualness while still with the universal.

Many in this earthly world have developed their minds to high levels of imagination and nonearthly awareness. We see it in how we grasp metaphors, emblems, and symbols, and in concepts and imagery that are beyond anything that is manifested in this physical reality. These powers flow from this pathway.

23 – The Sustaining Pathway

The "Sustaining Consciousness" (*Sekhel Kayam*) flows between the emanation of Splendor and Judgment. Here we gain the sustaining power necessary for the journey through the upper portions of the Tree of Life. Now we are moving into the higher heavens of vibration and consciousness. We need help. We find that help in this pathway. Once we are fully charged by the energy and awareness in this path, we are ready to move higher.

22 – The Faithful Pathway

Next is the "Faithful Consciousness" (*Sekhel Ne'eman*). It flows back and forth between Judgment and Beauty/Balance. A biblical passage refers to this level of consciousness and energy: "They will live again in God's shadow. They will grow like grain. They will blossom like grapevines. They will be as famous as the wines from Lebanon." (Hosea 14:7) Here we enjoy the blessings from God upon His faithful.

Kabbalah Study Guide – Van Auken

21 – The Pathway of Concilation

Next is the "Desired and Sought Consciousness" (*Sekhel HaChafutz VeHaMevukash*) through which flows the Divinity to and through us. Here we enjoy bestowing the blessings of God upon all of creation, as channels of God's grace to all. The object of our desire and seeking is realized, and we take a first step toward becoming the godly companions we were created to be by channeling God's blessings to others. Naturally, this flows between the emanation of Mercy and Loving Kindness and the emanation of Victory and Fortitude. This is also called the Path of Conciliation, where previous damage is repaired, where karma morphs into grace. Here all the harm we brought upon others is mended, and we become a blessing in the lives of others.

20 – The Pathway of Will

The pathway of "Consciousness of Will" (*Sekhel HaRatzon*) engages the most powerful gift given to us by our Creator: free will. As we find in the Scriptures: "Beloved, let us love one another; for love is of God, and he who loves is born of God and knows God. He who does not love does not know God; for God is love." –1 John 4:7-8

Now we willfully choose to love; we choose to share our consciousness with God and to be channels of God's emanations in whatever circumstance or relationship we find ourselves.

19 – The Spiritual Activities Pathway

Filled with the joy and inspiration of our journey so far, we reach the pathway of the "Consciousness of the Mystery of all Spiritual Activities" (*Sekhel Sod HaPaulot HaRuchniot Kulam*). Now we become aware of life in the Spirit and of all activities in the spiritual realms. We have arrived! We are ready to enter the highest heavens and do what godlings do throughout the Cosmos, free and alive. Since these are realms and activities so beyond anything we know on earth, they are a mystery to us. But we shall know them as we reach this level of enlightenment.

18 – The Influencing Pathway

Now we examine the "Consciousness of the House of Influences" (*Sekhel Bet HaShefa*). Here we intuit an allusion and probe a secret. Here we learn the forces behind the Cause of Causes, behind the First Motivation. These are among the highest level of vibration and awareness, having qualities of stillness and intuition.

17 – The Sensing Pathway

The "Consciousness of the Senses" (*Sekhel HaHergesh*) prepares the faithful seekers to be clothed in the "Spirit of Holiness." This is also called the Disposing Path, for it arranges, organizes, and marshals the energies and thoughts in a new order. We are truly changed and arrayed in ways we have not considered. At this level we are so close to God that it is becoming difficult to discern between ourselves and God, for we are nearly one.

16 – The Enduring Pathway

This is the pathway of the "Triumphal One," also known as the "Enduring Consciousness" (*Sekhel Nitzchi*). Those who endure wear the Crown of the triumph, and we are very close to the Crown now. There is no surer way of getting here than to keep on keeping on despite all obstacles. It is considered to be the "Delight of the Glory of God's Presence." It is also called the Garden of Eden, but this is the metaphysical garden that was prepared for the faithful.

15 – The Stabilizing Pathway

Finally, we reach the "Stabilizing Consciousness" (*Sekhel Ma'amid*), so called because it stabilizes the essence of creation in the "Glooms of Purity." Glooms of Purity is a strange concept. Kabbalists consider gloom to be a cocoon in which a metamorphosis from lonesome soul to untied godling magically occurs. This is similar to modern-day psychological belief that mild depression is a place of formative rebirth and creativity. One comes out of it with an intuitive sense of what to do next, yet went into it lost and uncertain. To find this place, outer life and consciousness must be a little gloomy, thus causing one to withdraw and to go deep within—there the magic happens, as in the cocoon.

14 – The Illuminating Pathway

This is a wondrous channel that flows between the emanations of Wisdom (Father) and Understanding (Mother). It is called "Illuminating Consciousness" (*Sekhel Meir*) because it is the essence of the "Speaking Silence" (*Chashmal*). It yields intuitive insights into the mysteries of the holy secrets.

13 – The Uniting Pathway

Here is the essence of the "Unity Directing Consciousness" (*Sekhel Manhig HaAchdut*). Here flows the balm of the completion of our truly unified spiritual being. It runs between the Crown and Beauty/Balance, and where else would we find such a healing union?

12 – The Glowing Pathway

From Understanding flows a pathway to the Crown and back again. It is called by the Kabbalists the "Glowing Consciousness" (*Sekhel Bahir*). It is thus called because it is the essence of the "Ophan-wheel of Greatness," as written in The Book of Enoch and seen by Ezekiel. It is called the "Visualizer" (*Chazchazit*), the place that gives rise to the Vision Seers, who can perceive the apparition of the Infinite Eternal (Ein Sof). It is also called the "Consciousness of Transparency," indicating that the veil between levels of consciousness no longer has the opacity to it with which we suffer in our limited inner vision.

11 – The Glaring Pathway

The final path is called "Glaring Consciousness" (*Sekhel MeTzuchtzach*), because of the brilliance of the Light of the "I AM." The hidden is exposed, the veil of the temple is rent, and the Holy of Holies is fully illuminated. Here we lose ourselves in the Holy Radiance of our Creator's presence. Kabbalists also call this the "Scintillating Consciousness," because its brilliance is more than a quality of light—it includes vibration and invigoration.

Now we might ask how one can apply all of these pathways in our daily lives. That would indeed be difficult if such pathways were linear and sequential, as our numbering and writing would imply, but they are operating simultaneously in a holistic manner. And, as we seek, they respond by naturally flowing to us. It is God's great pleasure to bless us with these energies and awarenesses.

Kabbalah Study Guide – Van Auken
SECTION 2 PART I
5 Divisions of Our Being

As you can see in the illustration, there are portions of the Tree of Life and the Emanations of God within our body temple and in our mental-emotional realms, and then in our higher heavenly, godly dimensions above the body. As you can also see it is quite natural that the Moral Triad is in our mental-emotional zone (brain, especially the large frontal lobe of our brain is where our its higher functions occur, especially higher moral functions) and the Mundane Triad is in our physical body vessel for a sojourn of some 80 to 100 years only, then we're back into the celestial parts of our consciousness. We are indeed Celestial Beings temporarily incarnating in a terrestrial reality for the purpose of soul growth and love. And even while we're incarnate in a body the higher celestial dynamics are with us, "above" us, and are accessible through introspection, meditation, and deep sleep visioning.

In Kabbalah the are 5 Major Divisions of Being
- Spirit Being (*Yechidah*)
- Spirit Mind (*Chayah*)
- Soul Being (*Neshamah*)
- Soul Mind (*Ruach*)
- The Living Being (*Nefesh*)

Over the past many years, books have been published recounting hospital near-death testimonials that have contributed to our understanding of life while the body is dead. Of course, the testimonials come from those whose bodies were resuscitated, but the accounts are amazingly similar to one another. Each patient experienced existence outside their dead body, and each saw imagery of loved ones who had died previously as well as realms of light and activity. Then, when the chemistry, electricity, and physical manipulation were sufficient to revive their body, they felt themselves drawn back into their body and this world, as if traveling rapidly through a long tunnel. Bang! They awoke on the operating or emergency room table with bright lights glaring at them.

Can we imagine this nonphysical aspect of our being? Can we feel our being without a body? If so, then we are aware of our higher nature, and this is much of what Kabbalah is about.

Ancient and modern philosophies and religions acknowledge various components of our whole being; most common is the simple body, mind, and spirit or soul arrangement. The ancient Egyptians identified five distinguishable parts to us, as does Kabbalah, although most teachers focus on the three aspects that are most present with us now.

These divisions are delineations of a oneness for the benefit of understanding and awareness, not a fixed condition. Oneness is the true, eternal condition; division is a temporary measure for the purpose of assisting us. We are whole, but consciousness and energy may be more focused in certain areas at any given time. Certainly in this realm, the physical is dominant for most people.

The ancient Bereishit Rabbah ("Great Genesis," a midrash, or homiletic study, section 14:9, on Genesis) speaks of five levels, or qualities, of our being. A problem occurs in that the five Hebrew words for these divisions are all translated in English as the same word: soul. And it does not help that three of the Hebrew terms are similar in their meaning: breath, wind, and breathing. We simply must understand that the distinctions are subtle, because we are talking about a wholeness of being. Even so, the distinctions are helpful to our understanding.

In a wonderful metaphor and using some of the imagery in the *Zohar*, Kabbalists Shim'on Lavi (1492-1585, an old guy for those times, ninety-three, although Shim'on Lavi may have actually been a father-and-son team by the same name) and Moshe Cordovero (1522-1570) compared these parts of our being to a glassblower, one who creates a beautiful, projected object by blowing through a pipe with molten glass on the end until the glass object is formed and then cuts the object from the pipe so that it sits on its own. In this metaphor, the glassblower's essence is our highest level of being, the glassblower is the next level, the breath of the glassblower is the third level, next is the expressed breath of the glassblower through the pipe that forms the glass and finally, the breath inside the glass object is the last level of our being—it is as the breath inside our physical body, the glass object our physical body.

Let's begin at the physical level which we know so well and then move to the highest level of our being. The first three parts are the only ones involved with the physical body. These are (1) the Living Being (Nefesh), (2) the Soul Mind (Ruach), and (3) the Soul Being (Neshamah). The higher two levels, (4) the Spirit Mind (Chayah) and (5) the Spirit Being (Yechidah) do not reside in the body. Yes, there is a portion of each of us that has not touched this world or our physical body.

KABBALAH
A Resource for Soulful Living

5 Divisions of Our Being

1. **Spirit Being** (Yechidah)
2. **Spirit Mind** (Chayah)
3. **Soul Being** (Neshamah)
4. **Soul Mind** (Ruach)
5. **Living Being** (Nefesh)

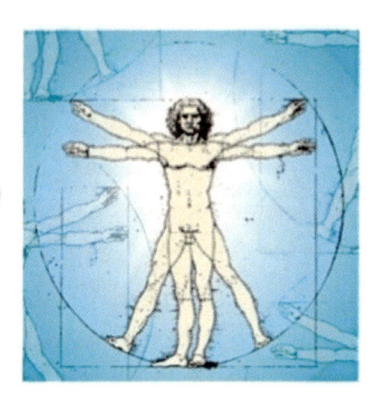

Copyright 2010 © by John Van Auken

KABBALAH
A Resource for Soulful Living
5 Divisions of Our Being

The *Great Genesis* ("Bereshit Rabbah" 14:9) speaks of five levels or qualities of our being. A problem occurs in that the five Hebrew words for these divisions are all translated in English as the same word: *soul*. And it does not help that three of the Hebrew terms are similar in their meaning: *breath*, *wind*, and *breathing*. We simply must understand that the distinctions are *subtle*, because we are talking about aspects of the *wholeness* of the being.

Copyright 2010 © by John Van Auken

KABBALAH
A Resource for Soulful Living
5 Divisions of Our Being
The Glassblower

In the metaphor of the glassblower, the *essence* of the artist is our highest level of being. The *entity* that is the glassblower is the next level. The *breath* of the glassblower is the third level. The *expressed* breath of the glassblower through the pipe that *forms* the glass object is the next level. And finally, the breath *inside the object* is the last level of our being.

—from the Zohar

Copyright 2010 © by John Van Auken

Details of the Five Major Divisions
The Living Being (Nefesh)

Translating the Kabbalah term Nefesh is easy, but understanding its meaning in this context is tricky. It means "breath," but as the glassblower metaphor indicates, it is the breath inside form, inside

40

the glass object, which is the body. Kabbalah considers this portion to be the "Living Being," in the sense of a "breathing creature" encased in form. Notice that the form is not the creature; rather, the creature is inside the form. This portion was the second Creation, which occurred in Genesis 2, not the first one, which occurred in Genesis 1, in the image of God. Here is the passage related to this Creation: "And the Lord God made man from the dust of the earth, breathing into him the breath of life, and man became a living soul." (Genesis 2:7) The word man in this passage is actually the Hebrew word adam, with a lowercased a, not the name Adam that is later used but the Hebrew word that means "beings" or "persons." The word adam has the connotation of being reddish in color, resulting from the reddish flush of life-giving blood in this being. What is most disappointing is that in the biblical book of Numbers (considered to be the fourth book of Moses), the term adam is always translated as "persons" (Numbers 31:28, 30, 35, 40, 46), while the Hebrew word *ish* is used to mean "male" or "man" (Numbers 1:4 and throughout). But, in Genesis, adam is translated as "man" instead of "persons," leaving us with a misconception that the first being was masculine.

These beings were formed from the dust of the earth, and the breath of life was breathed into them. Here the translators use the masculine pronoun "him," despite the fact that, at this point in the Creation (Genesis 2:7), the being contained both feminine and masculine qualities—it was androgynous! The separation of the gender qualities did not occur until later, in 2:21. The reason for the separation of the genders was that, in this new realm of duality (life and death, good and evil, night and day, yin and yang), where the heavenly oneness is now separated into individual bodies (one soul to a body), the beings were alone inside separate bodies, and they were lonely:" Then the Lord God said, 'It is not good that the man [adam=being or person] should be alone; I will make him a helper fit for him.'" (Genesis 2:18; RSV) But no helper that was fit for this level of being was found among all the creatures in this new dimension, so God took a portion from within the beings and made the companion.

"The man [beings] gave names to all cattle and to the birds of the air and to every beast of the field; but the man [beings] had no one like himself as a help. And the Lord God cast a deep sleep upon the man [beings], and took a rib [*tsela* means a "side" of its whole nature, not just a rib] from him while he was sleeping, joining up the flesh again in its place. And from the rib [side] which the Lord God had taken from the man [beings] he made a woman [*ishshah*, pronounced *ish-shaw* is female], and took her to the man [*ish* is male]." Genesis 2:20-22

Another important detail of this Creation is that there were actually two creations of the feminine. The first was Lilith and the second was Eve. Curiously, Edgar Cayce's readings state that there were also two Edens. The first one was in Poseidia, Atlantis, the birthplace of Lilith, and the second was the biblical Eden between the Tigris and Euphrates rivers, in what is today modern Iraq, the birthplace of Eve. This idea of an initial companion that preceded Eve is found in the writings of many early Jewish writers. There are also ancient depictions of Lilith. In Cayce's chronology, the first Eden, with Lilith, occurred roughly a hundred thousand years before Eve's Eden.

We should note that when we properly translate the term adam as "persons," even "humankind" as a whole, we find the answer to the age-old question of how Cain could have found a wife, when the previous passages give the impression that the earth only had Adam, Eve, and Abel for Cain to choose from! The term adam indicates that the Creator used the dust of earth and the breath of life to create humankind, not just one person, and certainly not one male, from which a little rib was taken to create his companion.

It is also important that we realize that humankind was created twice, once in the image of God (Genesis 1:26) and once from the dust of the earth (Genesis 2:7). This is the origin of the idea that we have a dual nature: divine and human, godly and earthly, spirit and flesh, essence and form, energy and matter. Next, we must realize that we, as godlings, have been diminished further through the separation of the gender qualities that were originally combined, naturally one, in every soul. A male is projecting only half of his whole soul being, and a female, only half of hers.

As we are now on the ascent of our soul journey through matter, it is natural that, for many years now, men have been struggling to get in touch with their feminine side and women have been struggling to get in touch with their masculine. It is only natural, because the soul self is both feminine and masculine.

Let's move on to the animal nature of this portion of our being. This fifth and lowest part of our being influences and is influenced by the bodily instincts, our animal nature, which contains all the base urges, cravings, and desires of bodily existence. But here also is our human nature, with its three-dimensional mind and personality, so shaped by our cultural and socioeconomic upbringing and genetic makeup. The animal and human nature compose our earthly Living Being. It is a thing apart from the heavenly, divine portions of our being.

Even when not incarnate, the cravings and habit patterns of this portion possess us, like a ghost that still desires physical sensation. Remember, the creature is inside the body, not the body itself, so even after the death of the body, this aspect of our being continues to influence us.

This "Living Being" is a dynamic that needs to be subdued, trained, and directed. Hinduism depicts this portion as a charioteer with the reins of the five stallions of the physical senses, which want to run wide and free! If the charioteer restrains self-seeking, self-gratifying impulses, then he or she opens the door to higher consciousness.

This lowest portion of our being is symbolized in the biblical character of Cain, whose name in Hebrew means "acquired" (from the Hebrew verb *qana* and explained by Eve herself in Genesis 4:1, "I have acquired one with the help of the Lord."). This is an acquired aspect of our total being. It is willful, self-centered, self-seeking, and not perfected, as reflected in Cain's character. God says to this aspect of our being, as to Cain: "Sin is crouching at the door [of your heart and mind]; its desire is for you, but you must master it." (Genesis 4:7) Sin, in Kabbalah, is imbalance and disharmony, most often caused by rebelliousness among the free-willed forces of life. When Cain rules, Abel (meaning "breath" in Hebrew but with the connotation of vapor, implying something transitory) is killed!

Abel is replaced with Seth (in Hebrew, Sheth), this name implying a new appointment. Again, Eve explains her choice of the name: "God has appointed [*shath*, meaning "replaced"] me another offspring...." (Genesis 4:25) Seth is the ancestor of Noah, whose generations repeople this part of the world after all the evil ones are cleansed by the Great Flood. Cain's progeny has moved far from Eden to the Land of Nod, east of Eden, which is modern-day Afghanistan. Cain is buried south of Kabul, Afghanistan. Isn't it interesting that we find ourselves back in the lands of Nod (Afghanistan) and Eden (Iraq), and struggling over the Holy City of Jerusalem? Yet these involvements indicate that we are on our return path whence we came.

This acquired outer self has become so dominant that we assume it to be our whole being—who we feel we are—the rest of our being having fallen into our unconsciousness.

Our outer being, this Living Being, is very much affected by the body's condition and its physical surroundings. The mental portion inside the body needs the body to be properly assimilating nutrients and eliminating toxins that build up. Our outer being also needs to turn within to find the true light, love, and life. However, the inner path is often perplexing to the outer self. The inner path does not fit within the three-dimensional model of life.

This brings us to our three-dimensional selves and our search for higher dimensions beyond our reality. We now understand that the higher dimensions are not in the third dimension. We must experience an altered state of perception. Nothing in the projected, three-dimensional reality will lead us to the fourth dimension. What is more perpendicular to an object-oriented being than venturing within itself? We must move from objects to thoughts and mental images within our minds. These are the "things" of the next dimension. Consider that they have no physical form, no projected shape, yet they have substance. Their form is not matter but the energetics of thoughts, imagery, and feelings are very real to us. It is not a physical cube but the thought form and feeling of it that is fourth-dimensional.

Grandmother's body may have died, but her deeper mind and core energetics live on; thus we can feel her, even see her with our deeper, dreaming mind's eye.

The mental dimensions are higher dimensions than the physical, 3-D dimensions of form, and they are powerfully creative and causal, as in this Scripture: "As one thinks in his heart, so is he." –Proverbs 23:7

The inner dimensions are as real and potent as the outer. The outer self must seek within to know these higher dimensions.

This naturally leads us to the next level of our being: the soul mind.

Soul Mind (Ruach)

Our Soul Mind—Ruach (from *ruah*, for wind or air)—is the moral consciousness that may subdue the urges and patterns of the Living Being. Here we have the ability to distinguish between good and evil, to subdue the most powerful instinctual urges for reasons higher than the gratification of these urges. This is the discerning mind and conscience. It is the involved mind that analyzes and correlates desires and measures them against the entity's deepest ideals. It is the expressed breath or "wind" of the glassblower. It is with us inside this projected experience (the glass).

This is also the portion of us that is the dreamer. When we are in this portion, we feel perfectly comfortable. We are ourselves. However, there is a subtle yet opaque veil separating this deeper mind from the outer consciousness. We know these two aspects of ourselves well. For example, each of us has had the experience of waking from an attention-getting dream, only to notice that the bladder is full, so we get up to empty the bladder, then return to the bed to review the dream—but it's gone! We have none of the content of the dream that so captured our attention just moments ago. How is this possible? It is possible because we have just experienced these two parts of ourselves: the Soul Mind, which dreamed the dream, and the Living Being, which accommodated the full bladder but did not dream the dream. So subtle is the veil between these two that we don't even notice when we move through it, yet, it is so opaque that we cannot see back through the veil. That is, unless we learn to. Then the veil becomes much more transparent, and we become more sensitive to subtle shifts in states of consciousness.

Kabbalah Study Guide – Van Auken

The Soul Mind is the subconscious, but with a much greater expanse than we normally give to the subconscious. This aspect of our being is tightly integrated with our outer mind (the conscious mind) and our body. One of the common communication channels between these two parts is dreaming. Many dreams that come to us are correlating of the development of our outer mind and body with ideals and aspirations of our soul and subconscious. This incarnation is as important, if not more important than it is to our outer self.

Inner life goes on in a manner reflective of how it occurs in the outer physical, material plane.

Soul life and consciousness are not far from physical life, and relationships extend beyond the separation that occurs when a body dies. This requires that we awaken to our Soul Mind, develop an awareness of the veil that separates us, and learn how to transform the veil's opacity to transparency. As we do this, we become aware of our next higher Self! This self is beyond the personality that we know in the projected life in physicality.

Soul Being (Neshamah)

Our Soul Being—Neshamah (from *nasham*, meaning "to breathe")—is our soul self, the ghost self of our whole being. It is the bridge between the physical incarnation and the heavenly tiers of our being. It is both in the body and beyond it. This is the portion of our being that is striving to save the Living Being from the wheel of desire and karma, to free it from its servitude to self-seeking entanglements. This is the breath of the glassblower.

These first three divisions are often considered to be the human being. As such, it is developing, changing, and ever moving toward earthlyness or toward heavenliness, often somewhere in between. The body is its temple and is either filled with the fires of self-seeking and gratification or the incense of love, kindness, and helpfulness toward others, and a sense of the godly connection and destiny. In many cases, there is a battle waging between these two opposing interests. Living Being (Nefesh) is often pulling in one direction and Soul Being (Neshamah) in the other. The Soul Mind (Ruach) is analyzing and correlating the activities and thoughts, giving its conscientious insights to help minimize the struggle—leading the two toward a cooperative effort to make the most of the immediate incarnation. Body, mind, and soul are commonly understood to be parts of our being and are comparable to Living Being, Soul Mind, and Soul Being. Let's now move beyond these and consider two portions of our being that are not common: Spirit Mind and Spirit Being. These are significant concepts in Kabbalah.

Spirit Mind (Chayah)

Our Spirit Mind—Chayah (the "living one")—is beyond anything earthly. It relates to the first flash of consciousness and the Giver of the gift of consciousness. Here is our spiritual mind, the womb of individual creativity, from which we use our very own free will to conceive. This level of our being can give life, can return life after illness or even death, and can "quicken" us, as is often said of the Spirit.

This is the glassblower. This is our divine consciousness. The glassblower's breath (Soul Being), its expressed breath (Soul Mind), and its encased breath (Living Being) journey out to experience the universe and the freedom of individual life.

This Spirit Mind maintains contact with the perfection of the Creator and the Creator's consciousness. It is the same yesterday, today, and tomorrow.

We can lift up lower portions of ourselves (soul mind and soul being) into this portion, but Spirit Mind does not normally descend to our level. And when it does, it is profoundly overwhelming to our soul mind and barely perceivable by our conscious mind.

Though it rarely descends, we can lift up our soul and Soul Mind up to it. Once the connection is made, we gain access to and help from the powerful Spirit Mind. But it is important to remember that the Spirit Mind has nothing earthly or worldly in it. Soul Mind is the savior, understanding the weaknesses of the Living Being. Spirit Mind is absolute truth with no room for vagaries.

When in the Spirit Mind, we would not perceive activity as we do in a dream of the Soul Mind. In the Spirit Mind, the imagery is more like a vision. It would be images like those the prophets described when seeing heavenly things, wondrous features, and dynamic energies.

Our subconscious mind is as the superconsciousness to our outer, conscious mind. But when the outer, conscious mind is subdued or absorbed into the higher mind, the subconscious becomes the active consciousness and the superconscious is as the subconscious is to us today in our present condition.

This may seem unnecessarily confusing, but it is really helpful when one is attempting to make passage through dimensions of consciousness. For example, when meditating, we must still the conscious mind and personality and all the concerns of the earthly portion of our being. As we do this, our soul mind and soul being become our natural condition of beingness—we are a soul. If we stay with the meditation, then we may move even deeper by subduing our soul self and awakening to our spirit mind, which is connected to God's mind. Now we are entering the deepest levels of meditation. This process also occurs in deepest sleep when visions rather than dreams come.

An illustration of this is found the in Revelation, chapter 19, when John, deep into his ecstasy, sees an angel in heaven. The angel gives him information, after which John falls down to worship the angel, believing it to be God's projection. The angel balks at this, saying, "You must not do that! I am your fellow servant and your brother....Worship God."(Revelation 19:10) When Peter and John were arrested, Peter was to be executed and John exiled to the Isle of Patmos. As they parted, Peter told John that he would endeavor to come to him after his death. Cayce says that, where he had his famous vision. As they parted, Peter told John that he would endeavor to come to him after his execution—this angel was Peter in the higher, superconscious quality of being, and as such, he appeared to John as an angelic expression of the Lord (remember, a portion of us was made in the image of God). That is why the angel says that he is the brother of John in this spiritual quest, and directs him to worship the God of all the godlings.

Spirit Being (Yechidah)

Our highest level of being is Spirit Being—Yechidah (meaning the "single one"). Here is the ultimate unity of the individual in God, as an individual spirit within and one with the Great Spirit. The Spirit Being is the highest of the five levels of being. It is the one made in the image of God. (Genesis 1:26) Here we also find that the superconscious mind is one with the Universal Consciousness of the Creator.

We have three basic levels of mind: physical consciousness, soul subconsciousness, and spirit superconsciousness. The physical is far from the spiritual, but the soul bridges this gap, connecting all of our parts—from the highest to the lowest and back again. There are also three distinct qualities of being: our outer projected self, our inner soul self, and our infinite spiritual self.

Kabbalah Study Guide – Van Auken

Levels of Being and the Chakras

Ancient mystical teachings associate the four lower chakras—root, navel, solar plexus, and heart—with the Living Being (Nefesh). These chakras are also associated with the four children of Horus in Egyptian mysticism, as well as the four beasts in Ezekiel, in Daniel, and in the Revelation. The three higher chakras—throat, third eye, and crown—would be associated with the Soul Mind (Ruach) and the Soul Being (Neshamah).

Many classical teachings associate the throat chakra with the will, and thus the first step to reconnecting with heavenly awareness and oneness with God. As one subdues his or her personal will and seeks God's will, one turns from this outer, lower reality to the inner, higher ones. The crown and third eye are luminaries of higher consciousness and renew energy in the body. This energy flows from heavenly realms through the crown (the soft spot in the head of our body as infants). When flowing, it opens the closed third eye, the mind's eye. This is also the region of the large frontal lobe of our brain, which so distinguishes us from animals. This area contains most of the dopamine-sensitive neurons associated with reward, attention, long-term memory, planning, and drive. In the frontal lobe resides the ability to conceive of future consequences resulting from current actions, to choose between good and bad actions, to recognize the best choice from among several options, to override and suppress unacceptable social responses, and discern similarities and differences between things or events.

Meditation improves one's bodily condition and raises one's level of consciousness. Drawing up the energy and consciousness from the lower chakras to the higher ones, is method for achieving higher vibrations and consciousness. Yoga aligns the flow of the kundalini straight up the spine to the crown of the head, but other ancient teachings in India, Egypt, and the Mayan lands teach that the energy and consciousness rise up from the base of the spine to the base of the brain; then to the center of the brain, where the crown chakra awakens (the soft spot); and then flows over to the great frontal lobe, where the hypothalamus and pituitary glands (the master glands of the body) are located. This pathway is reflected in the image of a winged cobra or other serpent in the striking position.

Interestingly, Edgar Cayce associated the seven chakras with the body's seven endocrine glands, which secrete their hormones directly into the blood system. The root chakra corresponds with the gonads (testes in males, and ovaries in females), the navel with the Leydig cells, the solar plexus with the adrenal glands and pancreas, the heart with the thymus, the throat with the thyroid, the crown with the pineal, and the third eye with the pituitary gland.

More on all of this in the lesson ecstasy and spiritualizing body, mind, and soul.

The Origin of Evil

The three lower aspects of being—Soul Being, Soul Mind, and Living Being—existed long before we ever contacted the third dimension and physical life, indicating that original sin was not a sin of the flesh, as is so often taught, but occurred in the spirit, in the soul, before it entered physical life. Souls brought their lower urges with them; flesh did not cause these urges, but it certainly facilitated a heightened expression of them.

Kabbalah teaches the same idea. When there is sin, darkness, or a defect in the Creation, it is caused by a separation of what should be united. Souls may become, by misuse of their free wills, so completely focused on themselves that they become separated from the Whole. Of course, there really is no way that we can be outside of the Whole, but we can become unconscious of our oneness with the Whole. When this occurs, the mediating flow between the Creator and the created is broken, disrupting the creative flow and bringing darkness, evil, illness, and a sense of separation and aloneness. Even angels fall when this occurs.

The Counter to Evil

However, there is a countering influence to this separation. Kabbalah teaches that the higher aspects of our being, Spirit Mind and Spirit Being, are as pure and perfect as the moment they were conceived by God in God's image. These higher portions have never left the presence and "throne of the Most High." Even the least among us has his or her pure being in God's presence.

The *Zohar* teaches that only the Nefesh is capable of sin. But that sin occurred before carnal life. This is why so many spiritual teachers purport that sin occurs in the heart and mind before it is manifested in the life of the body.

Then the simplest way to restore balance and well being is to go within and reconnect with our higher self. The reunion prepares the way for redemption and restoring wholesomeness.

Changing the Name of God

Let's conclude by once again reviewing stages of our Creation as expressed by changes in the name for God.

The Scriptures begin, *breshit bara elohim*, "In the beginning God...." The first name for God, as seen is this first line of Genesis, is Elohim. It is a plural Hebrew word that may be interpreted as "the Deities," and the verse about creating us is translated in the plural as well : "Let us make man in our image, after our likeness." (Genesis 1:26) By using the plural form, the authors were likely attempting to convey the collective nature of the Creator, to keep us from thinking that God is a divine individual, projecting individuals in its image, and that God is in some way a separate Being from us. Rather, it is a collective consciousness within which all the Creation was conceived and in which all exists. Elohim may be likened to the great assembly spoken of in Psalm 82:1, indicating all exists within this collective: "God is in the assembly of God; he is judging among the gods." Curiously, though, when this plural name is used, it is commonly construed with singular verbs and adjectives, adding to the belief that this is not polytheism but the collective nature of God. Before we leave this psalm, consider verse 6:"I said, 'You are gods, all of you are sons [and daughters] of the Most High.'" This is clearly a reference to our highest level of being, the Spirit Being with the Spirit Mind.

Kabbalah uses another name for the highest of God's qualities, a name that does not appear in any Scripture. It is Ein Sof, meaning the Infinite Eternal. It is beyond and all-inclusive of the creation and the multiplicity of manifested life.

As the Creation progresses, the name of God is changed. Changing the name of the God reflects changes in our relationship to God, not God's changing condition. God is unchanged. Originally, we were created in God's image, in Elohim's image. (Genesis 1:26) Then, in chapter two, Yahweh Elohim (often interpreted as "Lord God") creates us out of the dust of the earth and breathes life into us. (Genesis 2:7) In chapter four, Yahweh (Lord) is used during and after the birth of Cain and Abel. As the Bible story continues, God is called Adonai (Master), El (Mighty One), El 'Elyon (Most High God), El Shaddai (God Almighty), El 'Olam (Everlasting God), El Hai (Living God), and Avinu ("Our Father," as found in Isaiah 63:16; Jeremiah 31:9; Psalms 103:13; and 1 Chronicles 29:10). In the New Testament, Jesus continues the Jewish concept of God as Father, using Abba ("Father" in Aramaic and in colloquial Hebrew at the time of Jesus).

All of these names reveal our shifting relationship with God as we grow away or toward oneness with our Creator. Consider how God identified Him-Herself to Moses on the mount when answering Moses's question about His name: "I am that I am."

And Moses said unto God, "Behold, when I come unto the children of Israel, and shall say unto them, the God of your fathers hath sent me unto you; and they shall say to me, What is his name? What shall I say unto them?" And God said unto Moses, "I AM THAT I AM"; and he said, "Thus shalt thou say unto the children of Israel, I AM hath sent me unto you." Exodus 3:13-14

Why the Lower Levels of Being?

In the Garden, after eating from the Tree of the Knowledge of Good and Evil, Adam and Eve hid from God because they felt naked in God's all-knowing presence. Now there was no way they could be outside of the Whole or beyond God's all-knowing consciousness, but out of love for them, God developed the illusion of time and space and privacy. In this way they would feel that they had time to become comfortable in God's presence; they would have a sense of their private realm of imperfection until they could become cleansed and perfect again. The projected, lower, outer mind and being was this opportunity. It was symbolized by God making clothes for Adam and Eve and by their leaving the Garden of God's immediate presence. The lower divisions of our being gave us the time and space to use our wills to choose life over death, good over evil, and eventually feel comfortable in the All-Knowing's presence. The separation that we sought eventually becomes a thing of the past as we resolve our discomfort in the presence of the All-knowing. That which had become separated is thus united again.

SECTION 2 PART 2
4 Planes of Our Existence

We touched on this earlier but now let's go into detail on this important Kabbalah concept.

In Kabbalah life exists in four distinct planes, and these planes of existence are best thought of as concentric circles expanding out from a center, singular source. These two diagrams illustrate this view, each with a slightly different view (remember, Kabbalah was understood by different cultures and traditions).

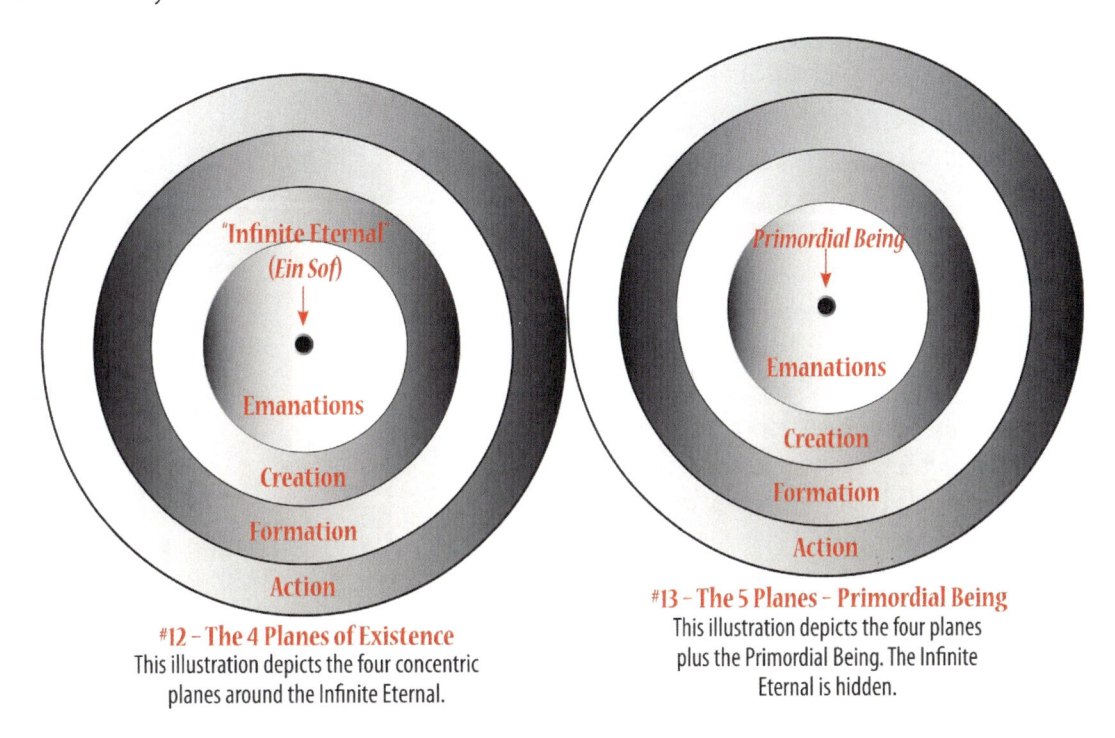

#12 – The 4 Planes of Existence
This illustration depicts the four concentric planes around the Infinite Eternal.

#13 – The 5 Planes – Primordial Being
This illustration depicts the four planes plus the Primordial Being. The Infinite Eternal is hidden.

As we study these keep in mind that they coexist within us (microcosm) and around us (macrocosm). The illustration on the next page reveals how they exist within us.

See the planes in red ink: Emanation, Creation, Formation, and Action.

The universe we know is not the first one to have been created, but it is the longest lasting, according to Kabbalistic tradition—and for a good reason. The Creator desired to create companions, companions that chose to be so, thus they had to have free will. These potential companions would also need to grow into their role, gradually becoming fully aware of the life forces flowing through all of creation as well as all that is concealed in the depths of the Infinite Womb. None of this growth and learning would be possible if God's perfect nature permeated the entire universe, so God withdrew a portion of Itself to allow for the imperfections of Its developing companions, using freedom and choice to grow into their potential. Fortunately, the all-wise Creator established a very effective law to control the possibility for chaos; that law is what we know today as karma: As we sow with our free will, we experience; and as we measure out to others, so it is measured back to us. This law was not established to mete out punishment or retribution, as so many teach, but to provide our souls with the enlightenment and education of experiencing the effects of our free-will actions and thoughts. The Creator's intent was to help each soul make better choices and become eternal companions to the Creator—consciously and interactively, even co-creators with the Great Creator.

Our wondrous potential is expressed in the Kabbalistic text Hekhalot Zutarti:

"What is the man that he is able to ascend upwards, to ride wheels, to descend downwards, to explore the world, to walk on dry land, to behold his radiance, ... [missing text here], his crown, to be transformed through his honor, to say praise, to combine signs, to say names, to peer upwards and to peer downwards, to know exactly the living and to behold the vision of the dead, to walk in rivers of fire and to know the lightning."

—Hekhalot Zutarti, Section 349

The *Zohar* provides a map of four different planes of consciousness, as do other treatises, old and new. We traverse these planes in our soul-growth journeys. Soul-life experiences occur on these planes, and we may actually have flashes of awareness of these four planes.

In Lurianic Kabbalah (a system containing Indian philosophy, Platonism, and Gnosticism), there are five planes of existence, because they add to the four basic planes the Primordial Being (Adam Kadmon) as a plane of consciousness all its own. This means that the archetype of the Primordial Being is another plane of experience in our soul growth. The Logos plane becomes a conduit into the Infinite, Ineffible God.

Before we learn about the planes, let's briefly discuss the Hebrew word *Olam*. Most agree that the word relates to both distance and time, in the sense of "a far distance" and "a long time." It is so very hard to take our three-dimensional framework and stretch it to grasp fourth, fifth, and higher dimensional realities. Most writers have translated *olam* as "world" but agree that it could also mean "a plane of unimaginable distance and time." Even this definition is inadequate, because space and time only exist in our present reality—the third dimension. Fortunately, many of us have come to understand states of consciousness, degrees of awareness, and realms of perception. For example, we recognize the difference between a materialistic person, who mostly lives in the physical reality, as opposed to a person who has a mind that reaches far beyond physicality. We know people who perceive elements of musical experience far beyond normal people—thus possessing a level of perception beyond the norm. We know minds that comprehend the laws governing the universe, while others just live in it, not aware of what is involved. Today we grasp the concept of paradigms, archetypes, and mental constructs; theoretical frameworks of unseen influences upon reality are within our appreciation. All these ideas help us to grasp planes of soul existence and to interpret the word *olam* in broader understanding.

Now we might quickly use the term states of consciousness, except that the Cayce readings warn that even in higher dimensions, where the physical body is not manifested, there are magnetic-like forces that create vessel-like orbs of being for individual soul-mind entities—a type of "body." We might think of them as energy fields that form multidimensional bodies. Even so, these are not like the degree of encasement we experience in a physical body on earth, because the energy fields of our individual consciousness can expand into infinity and back again.

With all of this in mind, let's interpret olam as a plane of existence in which a personal consciousnesses with a bodylike concentration of "beingness" experiences life.

Four Planes

Plane of Emanation: On this plane the Expression of Life (of which we are a part) unites with the unseen Source of Life. Here we may know oneness with the Infinite Eternal (*Ein Sof*). This is the Celestial Triad of the emanations: I AM, Wisdom, and Understanding—from which all of the emanations are expressed.

Plane of Creation: This is also known as the plane of conception. That which came out of "the deep" expresses its quintessence. Here are the Creative Forces. This is the dimension of the Moral Triad of the emanations: Mercy, Judgment, and Beauty. This is the plane of the archangels and divine souls (*neshamot mekoriyyah*).

Plane of Formation: Here the unseen essences take form, in the sense of energies and consciousnesses, not bodies. This is the Mundane Triad of the emanations: Persistence (Victory), Surrender (Splendor), and Remembrance (Foundation). This is the plane of angels and the Orphanim (Never-sleeping Watchers/Guardians). Here we find the laws that shape the *patterns* of creation and form "the sevens": seven heavens, seven planets, seven chakras, seven ages, and so on.

Plane of Action: This is the physical realm where the created engage their wills to do as they desire and experience the result, experience the reaction—which we know to be karma. This is the plane of inferior and fallen angels and the broken vessels (*Kellipot*) that were not perfect enough to contain and pass along the Light of the I AM as it flowed out of the Infinite Eternal (*Ein Sof*). Here we find the four elements of the lower plane: solid/matter (earth), liquid/fluid (water), plasma (fire), and gas/vapor (air). In this realm we find the physical universe, particularly our galaxy, and the forces of the zodiac, the seven planets, the two great lights of the sun and moon, and the realm of testing: earth, the casual world.

Copyright 2010 © by John Van Auken

Kabbalah Study Guide – Van Auken

Here are the four planes that are common to most Kabbalistic texts and teachings. They are concentric circles of existence surrounding a point. The above illustrations help us grasp for the planes and the triads. Below is a bit more detail:

1. Plane of Emanation (Olam Atzilut)

The first realm of existence is the Plane of Emanations. On this plane the Expression of Life (of which we are a part) unites with the unseen Source of Life. Here we may know oneness with the Infinite Eternal (Ein Sof). This is the Celestial Triad of the emanations: I AM, Wisdom, and Understanding—from which all of the emanations are expressed.

This is the plane of the powers of God, the Divine Visages (*partzufim*), and the Brilliant Light. Here is the realm of the Infinite God, the Omnipotent, All-knowing, Universal Mind and Spirit. This plane is also known as the "Boundless World of Divine Names" and "Rings of Sacred Names." All of creation is in this plane but in its uncontamined state, pure as the moment it was divinely conceived. The perfection of this realm is not affected by what goes on in the lower realms; however, the ideal of this perfection is in all the realms below it.

Here the ten emanations of God are maintained as the Lights—pure and brilliant—eternal and untouched by the lower realms. To touch this realm or live in it is to be in ecstasy, bliss, nirvana, samadhi, and all the other terms humans have used to describe this peace that passes understanding and yields complete contentment. One is what one was meant to be.

2. Plane of Creation (Olam Briah)

The second realm is the Plane of Creation, also known as the plane of conception. That which came out of "the deep" expresses its quintessence. Here are the Creative Forces. This is the dimension of the Moral Triad of the emanations: Mercy, Judgment, and Beauty. This is the plane of the archangels and divine souls (neshamot mekoriyyah). Here is the Lord of Hosts. The life essence of the Creator permeates this realm, giving goodness to all.

This plane is also known as the "Archangelic World of Creations," revealing that it is the dimension of the archangels who play a major role in the whole of creation.

In the first plane, the ten emanations of God are called Lights; in this plane they are called Spirits—divine beings who serve in the establishing of orders and intelligences throughout the seen and unseen universes.

3. Plane of Formation (Olam Yetzirah)

The third plane is the Plane of Formation. Here the unseen essences take form, in the sense of energies and consciousnesses, not bodies. This is the Mundane Triad of the emanations: Victory (Persistence) Splendor (Surrender), and Foundation (Remembrance). This is the plane of angels and the Orphanim (Never-sleeping Watchers/Guardians). Here we find the laws that shape the patterns of creation and form the sevens: seven heavens, seven planets, seven chakras, seven ages, and so on. Here we find the higher element of ether, or akasha in Sanskrit; this is the most subtle and expansive of the five elements.

Every thought, word, and action of every soul makes an impression upon the akasha and may be "read." This is the Book of Life of each soul.

Here the ten emanations of God are called the "Hierarchies of Celestial Beings," sometimes referred to as Choirs.

4. Plane of Actions (Olam Asiyah)

The fourth plane is the Plane of Actions. It is the physical realm where the created engage their wills to do as they desire and experience the result, experience the reaction—which we know to be karma. This is the plane of inferior and fallen angels and the broken vessels (*Kellipot*) that were not perfect enough to contain and pass along the Light of the I AM as it flowed out of the Infinite Eternal (Ein Sof). Here we find the four elements of the lower plane: solid/matter (earth), liquid/fluid (water), plasma (fire), and gas/vapor (air). In this realm we find the physical universe, particularly our galaxy, and the forces of the zodiac, the seven planets, the two great lights of the sun and moon, and the realm of testing: earth, the casual world.

This plane is also called the "Elemental Plane of Substance."

In this plane the ten emanations of God are called "Shells" (Kellipot). This is also the realm of demons, tempters, and distortions. The shells and demons are listed as the dark, or shadow, side and consist of the "Twins of God" (Thaumiel), the "Two-Headed" (doubled-mindedness, wanting God and mammon), Satan, Moloch (the impious god of fire sacrifices), Adam Belial ("Wicked Being"), "Confusion of God's Power" (Chaigidel), "Those Who Go Forth into the Place Empty of God" (Ghogiel), Beelzebub ("Lord of Flies"), Lucifuge (opposite of Lucifer the Light Bearer, this name means "Flees the Light"), Devourers or Wasters (Gamchicoth), Destroyers (Golachab, Golab, and Usiel), "Builders of Ugliness" (Thagirion), Lord of Darkness (Baal), desolation (Samael), pollution (Gamaliel), and frightening sounds and strange desires (Nehemoth). These are the shells and demons that plague this realm. However, there are Light Forces battling these dark influences all the time—each struggling for the souls and minds of the incarnate.

This brings us to the forces of **"Repairing and Perfecting the Plane"** (Tikkun Olam). In Lurianic Kabbalah explains that the vessels that shattered because they could not contain and distribute the original Light of God, and their shards became sparks of light, are trapped within the material of creation. Contemplative prayer releases these sparks and allows them to reunite with God's essence, thus repairing this plane and restoring God's essence throughout the plane. This is the promised time in the biblical book of Revelation when Satan is bound and the earth goes through a golden age of no evil, no temptation, and God's essence is manifest in the material plane.

SECTION 2 PART 3
The Seven Heavens

In Kabbalah's arrangement there are these 7 heavenly realms. And as you can see, they expand as one ascends from finite awareness to infinite perception, from individuality to universality.

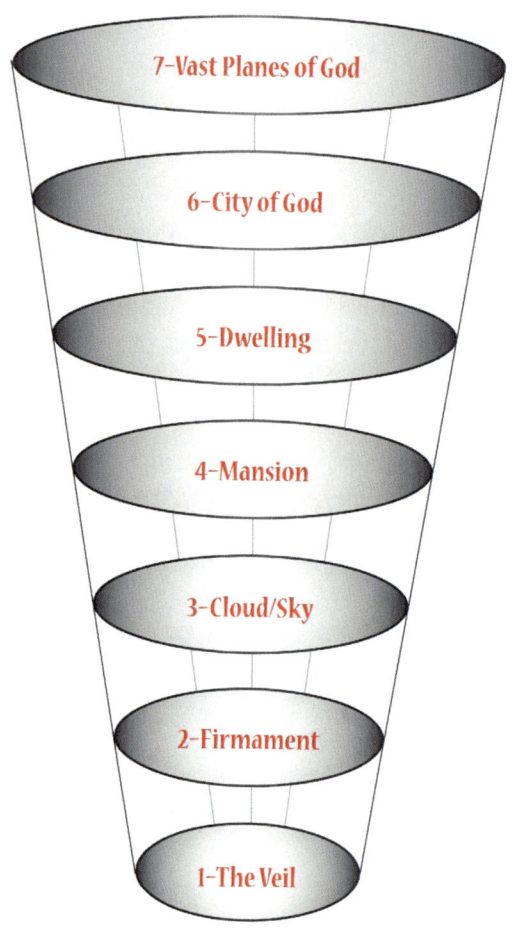

- 7 – Vast Planes of God
- 6 – City of God
- 5 – Dwelling
- 4 – Mansion
- 3 – Cloud/Sky
- 2 – Firmament
- 1 – The Veil

#15 – The 7 Heavens
The mystical initiate ascends through the seven heavens, one after another, using meditative practices.

"In the beginning God created the heavens and the earth."(Genesis 1:1 RSV,ASV,WEB) Clearly, the first line in three different translations of the Bible indicates that there are heavens, not simply a heaven. When a person says, "I was in seventh heaven," he means that he was the happiest he could be. "Seventh heaven" is expressed in Yiddish, zibnten himl. Kabbalah reveals these seven heavens, and even gives insight into how one may come to traverse them.

Merkabah mysticism, based on the visions of Ezekiel, Isaiah, and Daniel and found in Hekhalot writings, teaches the initiate to ascend to and through the heavens by meditation practices, passing from one to another, finally entering through the seven "palaces" in the seventh heaven to the very throne of God.

In contrast, the Hasidim (a pious movement originating in Poland and Ukraine) perspective teaches: "It is not the mystic who ascends through the palaces, but the relational aspect of God that descends to man."

From the perspective of a mystic, we are to lift ourselves up through the heavens to the Throne, because drawing heaven down to our level is a faltering way and does not help awaken us to our godly nature and destiny. Seekers tend to falter because they are ignorant of or ignored the teaching that we are gods—sons and daughters of the Most High—as in Psalm 82 and referred to by Jesus in the gospel of John 10:34.

There are Kabbalah texts teaching one how to achieve a heavenly ascent through the "heavenly palaces" (Hekhalot) and what to expect there. There are also Kabbalah texts teaching how one may draw down angelic spirits to interact with and help the seeker. Cayce's readings are not against this, but encourage seekers to let God send the guides and angels, for He knows best.

There are several larger documents of the Hekhalot (also spelled Heichalot), such as Hekhalot Rabbati (in which six of the seven palaces of God are described), Hekhalot Zutarti, Shiur Komah, and 3 Khanokh (which is also known as 3 Enoch, The Book of the Palaces, The Book of Rabbi Ishmael the High Priest, and The Revelation of Metatron). There are also hundreds of small documents, many little more than fragments, which address the concept of heavenly realms (palaces, firmaments, planes) and describe methods for traversing them (though this is very dangerous and requires much practice and skill—as well as a pure heart and a clear and focused mind).

Among various Gnostic groups and some early Christian ones, the meditative journey through the seven heavens was also known and practiced, always secretly.

The disciple Paul revealed this, too, when he wrote, "I know a man in Christ who fourteen years ago (whether in the body, I know not; or whether out of the body, I know not; God knows), was caught up even to the third heaven." (2 Corinthians, 12:2)

In the Koran, dictated to Mohammed by the archangel Gabriel, it is written, "See you not how Allah has created the seven heavens one above another, and made the moon a light in their midst and made the sun a lamp?" (Sura 71)

In most teachings of the Kabbalah, the seven heavens are listed, from lowest to highest, as in the following (see illustration on page 61):

1. Veil (Vilon)–the curtain, the veil of heaven (Vilon Shemaim); taken from Isaiah 40:22.
2. Firmament (Raki'a)–the firmament, the canopy, the expanse of heaven, which are the stars, moon, and sun; mentioned in Gen 1:14-18.
3. Cloud/Sky (Shehakim)–the clouds from which the manna from heaven fell to nourish the seekers. Here is where the well of the water of life is and the fountain of gardens; taken from Psalm 78:24-26.
4. Mansion (Zebul)–the lofty dwelling, "mansion of holiness" (zevul kodshekha), considered the temple-mansion in the "Golden City"; taken from 1 Kings 8:11-13.
5. Dwelling (Ma'on)–the refuge, a place of peace from the struggles. Home of the ministering angels; mentioned in Deuteronomy 26:15.
6. "City of God" (Makon)–the changeless, perfect residence, containing the template for all life forms. This is the storehouse of good, eternal treasures; taken from 1 Kings 8:39.
7. "Vast Plains of God" (Aravot)–the highest heaven, the vast expansive plains of God, Infinity, the Eastern "Void"; empty, still, silent, a dimension of pure contentment. This is the Divine Womb from which all life originally came into being; taken from Psalm 68:4.

Notice that the first three heavens are associated with physical life, the second three with mental dimensions of consciousness, and the last with Infinity, a quality that human beings would have difficulty knowing directly because of their finite nature. Yet, following a sequential passage through each of the dimensions during deep meditation the seeker can rise to a state of consciousness in the Infinite Mind of God. Even Cayce's teachings support this view and give a clear method for making such passage in consciousness.

In the Talmud, Rabbi Resh Lakish, one of the most famous scholars of the Torah, describes the seven heavens in some detail: "[There are] seven, namely: Wilon [Vilon], Rakia, Shehakim, Zebul [Zevul], Ma'on, Makon, Araboth [Aravot]. Wilon [Vilon] serves no purpose except that it enters in the morning and goes forth in the evening and renews every day the work of creation, for it is said: 'That stretches out the heavens as a curtain, and spreads them out as a tent to dwell in.'"

"Rakia is that in which sun and moon, stars and constellations are set, for it is said: 'And God set them in the firmament [Raki'a] of the heaven.'

"Shehakim is that in which millstones stand and grind manna for the righteous, for it is said: 'And He commanded the skies [Shehakim] above, and opened the doors of heaven; and He caused manna to rain upon them for food.'

"Zebul is that in which (the heavenly) Jerusalem [as described in the Revelation] and the Temple and the Altar are built, and Michael, the great Prince, stands and offers up thereon an offering, for it is said: 'I have surely built Thee a house of habitation [Zebul], a place for Thee to dwell in for ever.' And whence do we derive that it is called heaven?' For it is written: 'Look down from heaven, and see, even from Thy holy and glorious habitation.'

"Ma'on is that in which there are companies of Ministering Angels, who utter (divine) song by night, and are silent by day for the sake of Israel's glory, for it is said: "By day the Lord doth command His loving kindness, and in the night His song is with me."

"Araboth is that in which there are Right and Judgment and Righteousness, the treasures of life and the treasures of peace and the treasures of blessing, the souls of the righteous and the spirits and the souls which are yet to be born, and dew wherewith the Holy One, blessed be He, will hereafter revive the dead. There [too] are the Ofanim and the Seraphim, and the Holy Living Creatures, and the Ministering Angels, and the Throne of God; and the King, the Living God, high and exalted, dwells over them in Araboth, for it is said: 'Extol Him that rides upon Araboth whose name is the Lord....'" [note: the brackets and parentheses in these passages were in the original]

For you and me today the most important heaven is the lowest one, the Veil or Curtain, because if we can perceive it and develop a conscious awareness of it, then we have made the first big step toward total spiritual awakening and making passage through the 7 Heavens. Despite what you may think, we know this veil well and are familiar with the qualities of our mind on both sides of this veil. To again use a familiar example, how many times have we had a dream that impressed us (either scared us or inspired us), and as we came closer to waking, we noticed that our bladder was full, so we decided to go empty the bladder and then reflect on the dream when we returned? Yet, when we returned to our bed, the dream was completely gone! We had no recollection of it. How is this possible? We just experienced the veil, a most subtle yet opaque veil! When in the dream, we were in our soul mind and were quite comfortable there. We knew it as a part of ourselves. Then, as we engaged our body to walk to the bathroom, we passed through this veil into our outer mind, which is in charge of moving the body. However, our outer mind did not have the dream! It has no content of the dream, only a sense that the inner mind has content that is going to be reviewed. But it does not contain that content. Now we see just how subtle and yet opaque this veil is. We do not even notice when we pass through it, and yet, once on the other side, we cannot see back through it.

Fortunately, that's only partially true, because if we practice becoming more aware of subtle aspects of consciousness, we will come to perceive the movement through the veil and what side of the veil we are on at any given time. We will explore more on this in the final section of the book, on Spiritualization and Reunion. For now, let's keep in mind that these levels of heaven are levels of consciousness and that we can expand our consciousness as we awaken spiritually.

As crowded as earth is the heavens are much more crowded, as we will learn in the lesson on Angels, Archangels, and Demons. Despite this, any individual soul-mind can make passage through the heavens undisturbed. How? Again it is the amazing dynamic of the microcosm existing within the macrocosm. Within one's own consciousness all the heavens may be known personally, and with God's guiding help. Eventually, as one develops oneself, he or she may become ready to awaken to the macrocosm and the crowds of souls, beings, angels, and all the lifeforms existing in the Great Creation. (Note: I mean "lifeforms" in the sense of thought-forms, not physical beings. Again, real life exists in mind. And one has a personal mind and a mind within the Infinite Mind of God and all creation.)

Kabbalah Study Guide – Van Auken

KABBALAH
A Resource for Soulful Living
The 7 Heavens

1. **Veil** (*Vilon*)–the curtain, the veil of heaven (*Vilon Shemaim*); taken from Isaiah 40:22. [Sleep, etc.]
2. **Firmament** (*Raki'a*)–the firmament, the canopy, the expanse of heaven, which are the stars, moon, and sun; mentioned in Gen 1:14-18. [Mayan Tale]
3. **Cloud/Sky** (*Shehakim*)–the clouds from which the manna from heaven fell to nourish the seekers. Here is where the well of the water of life is and the fountain of gardens; taken from Psalm 78:24-26. EC:"Paradise." [Paul]
4. **Mansion** (*Zebul*)–the lofty dwelling, "mansion of holiness" (*zevul kodshekha*), considered the temple-mansion in the "Golden City"; taken from 1 Kings 8:11-13. "In my father's house are many mansions."
5. **Dwelling** (*Ma'on*)–the refuge, a place of peace from the struggles. Home of the ministering angels; mentioned in Deuteronomy 26:15. Psalm 46.
6. **"City of God"** (*Makon*)–the changeless, perfect residence, containing the template for all life forms. This is the storehouse of good, eternal treasures; taken from 1 Kings 8:39.
7. **"Vast Plains of God"** (*Aravot*)–the highest heaven, the vast expansive plains of Infinity, the Eastern "Void"; empty, still, silent, a dimension of pure contentment. This is the Divine Womb from which all life originally came into being; taken from Psalm 68:4.

Copyright 2010 © by John Van Auken

The 7 Heavens correlate to the 7 Lotuses of Consciousness within Us!

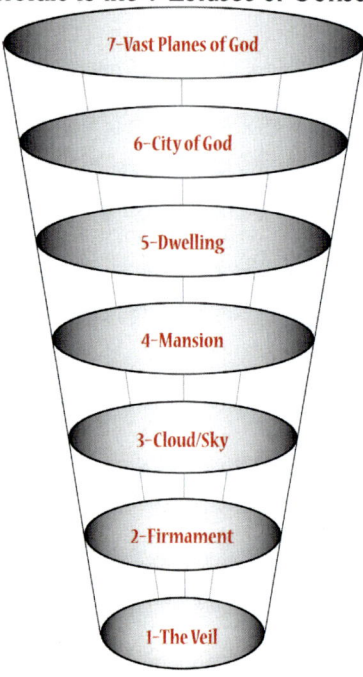

- 7-Vast Planes of God
- 6-City of God
- 5-Dwelling
- 4-Mansion
- 3-Cloud/Sky
- 2-Firmament
- 1-The Veil

#15 – The 7 Heavens
The mystical initiate ascends through the seven heavens, one after another, using meditative practices.

SECTION 3 PART 1
Angels, Archangels, and Demons

KABBALAH
A Resource for Soulful Living

Angels, Archangels, & Demons

St. Augustine wrote, "Every visible thing in this world is put under the charge of an angel." *Genesis Rabba* (a Jewish commentary on the biblical Genesis) states, "There's not a stalk on earth that has not its angel in heaven." According to Psalm 91:11, "God has charged his angels to watch over you," and Jesus confirms this in Matthew 4:11 and 26:53.

Copyright 2010 © by John Van Auken

KABBALAH
A Resource for Soulful Living

Angels, Archangels, & Demons

In the Old Testament, Yahweh is called "the Lord of hosts;" *hosts* being the legions of angels. Psalm 82:1 states that "God stands in the *Congregation* of God; He judges among the gods." Here the angels compose the congregation and are godlings within the one God.

Copyright 2010 © by John Van Auken

Kabbalah has a highly developed cosmology of heavenly beings, with a long history of their activities and influences. And once again we have that paradoxical reality of the macrocosm and the microcosm, meaning that these heavenly influences are with the psyche of each of us as well as outside of us in the universe.

Botticelli's Angels

On the other side of our earthly, human self is a divine portion of our being that is an angel! It is heavenly, has never left its original place with God, and was made in the image of God. This is the "holy immortal" portion of us, as described in Zoroastrian lore. For an example of how these three portions of our being interface, let's consider the biblical story of the patriarch Jacob, his twin brother, Esau, and the angel that Jacob wrestled as metaphors for these three parts of ourselves. Our earthly, personality self is played by Esau, a hunter and warrior, hairy and strong, wild and free, who loved the fields and woods of the earth. Jacob, on the other hand, represents our more internal and reflective nature—our soul self. Jacob was gentle, enjoyed learning and good conversation, liked the company of women and the surroundings of the tribal camp, and had developed a skill with domesticated animals, particularly husbandry of breeding healthy goats and sheep. Esau's persona sought to experience physical life with as much gusto as possible, whereas Jacob, as our deeper soul self, sought to experience the higher, ethereal things, more of the mind and heart than of the body. One night, in a profound experience, Jacob met an angel of the lord. He caught firm hold of the angel and would not let it go until the angel blessed him. After the blessing, Jacob asked the angel's name, and the angel was surprised by such a question and gave no answer. Could it be that the angel was none other than Jacob's divine self, his angelic self? After this experience, Jacob said that he had seen God "face to face." How could he make such a statement unless the angel was also before the throne of God? And by engaging this aspect of the whole "entity" (as Cayce liked to called us) Jacob had engaged his own angelic aspect that was intimately connected to God. We may consider this story an example of how our personality, soul, and angel self interact with one another.

In ancient Egyptian lore, we are composed of a three aspects: a ba, ka, and akhu, which may be translated as soul, "twin," and godling!

St. Augustine wrote, "Every visible thing in this world is put under the charge of an angel." Genesis Rabba (a Jewish commentary on the biblical Genesis) states, "There's not a stalk on earth that has not its angel in heaven." And according to Psalm 91:11, God has charged his angels to watch over us, as Jesus affirms in Matthew 4:11 and 26:53.

There was a time when only our angelic selves existed. The angelic part of our being was alive and active long before Earth, long before physical bodies. Life existed in the spirit, or we might say, in energy not matter. Perhaps if we think of ourselves as minds without form this may help awaken us to our angelic portion. The One Mind created within itself many individual consciousnesses and gave them free will. Life went along in this manner for many, many eons before some of these children of God transitioned their energy into matter. What was it like back then? What were the angels doing? Cayce and Kabbalah, along with many earth legends and fables, give us some of the amazing pre-Earth history. Let's explore some of the chronicles of the angels.

In the Old Testament, Yahweh is called "the Lord of hosts;" hosts being the legions of angels. We find this in Psalm 82:1, which states: "God stands in the Congregation of God; He judges among the gods." Here the angels compose "the Congregation" and we are the gods or godlings within the one God. Notice that the term Congregation of God implies that all in the congregation are godlike.

When speaking of angelic beings, the Bible uses the terms "messenger of God" (*melakh Elohim*), "messenger of the Lord" (*melakh Adonai*), "Sons of God" (*b'nai Elohim*), and the "Holy Ones" (*ha-qodeshim*). Other terms are used in later texts, such as the "Upper ones" (*ha'oleevoneem*).

Daniel is the first biblical figure to refer to individual angels by name, identifying the archangels **Michael** and **Gabriel** by name.

In Kabbalah, and other angel lore, **Metatron** is considered the highest of the angels. Metatron is briefly mentioned in the Talmud and figures prominently in Merkabah mystical texts. In 3 Enoch, or the "Book of Heavenly Palaces" (Sefer Hekhalot), there is a link between Enoch, son of Jared (great-grandfather of Noah), and his transformation into the angel Metatron. Surprisingly, there is the same connection in the Edgar Cayce readings! As strange as the name is, this is the highest angel in almost all listings of angels. We'll cover more on this angel in a moment.

Michael, who serves as a warrior and an advocate for Israel (Daniel 10:13), is considered to be the guardian angel of the Israelites, while Gabriel is the guardian of the Ishmaelites (modern-day Arabs). This began with the two sons of Abraham: Isaac and Ishmael. Gabriel is mentioned briefly in the Talmud, as well as in many Merkabah mystical texts.

In Jewish and Dionysian lore, the Congregation of Angels is arranged into two main choirs: **Seraphim** and **Cherubim**.

Seraphim are the highest order of angels and attend to the throne and altar of God. They are variously referred to as the burning ones, the red ones, and beings of fire, because of their association with the fire of the altar of God and the fire of truth, particularly the "test as by fire" that the archangel Michael requires of every soul who attempts to pass to higher levels of heaven. In the Bible, seraphs—mentioned only in Isaiah 6:2 and 6:6—surround the throne of God and bring Isaiah a coal from the fire on the altar of God with which to cleanse his lips and speech. Seraphs are often depicted with six wings. The colors red and white are associated with them, as well as the element of fire. Cayce's reading 275-35 actually refers to the "seraphim choir" when instructing a young man about his music training, noting that the "Prince of Peace was a harpist" in such a choir.

Cherubim, on the other hand, are mentioned throughout the Bible. Their name is derived from the Assyrian (or Akkadian) word kirubu, which means "one who prays, blesses, or intercedes," and are often seen as those who intercede between God and humans. As the second order of angels, they are often depicted as winged children, but this originated during the Middle Ages and is not a classical image of them. Cherubs are depicted as having four wings, and blue is the color associated with them, because of their connection with the sky and, in some cases, with the wind and the element of air. All the angels are active beings, much involved with the lives of humans. They were and are co-creators with the Creator, and as such, created much of the universe that we see. How many angels were created? According to the Egyptians, each star in heaven is the light of one specific angel, and there are more stars in the portion of the universe that is visible from earth than there are grains of sand on all the beaches and deserts of earth!

The 9 Choirs of Angelic Beings

The traditional order of the angelic hierarchy fits with the three Triads of the Tree of Life, and in each of the three Triads are three choirs of angels. Here is the order:

First Choirs
Seraphim - Cherubim - Thrones
Second Choirs
Dominations (Dominions) - Virtues - Powers
Third Choirs
Principalities - Archangels - Angels

• The **Seraphim** are the highest order of the nine choirs of angels. They surround the throne of God continually singing, "Holy, Holy, Holy is the God of Hosts!" They are said to be so bright that humans cannot look at them. Lucifer was among the Seraphim before the rebellion in heaven that led to his fall and that of many angels. The Prince of this choir is Michael.

• The **Cherubim** were God's choice for the Ark of the Covenant. Dionysius taught that these were the angels of knowing, or knowledge. They were assigned to guard the Tree of Life from humanity, less we eat from it and become immortal. (In Revelation this restriction is rescinded, allowing spiritualized humans to eat the fruit of the Tree of Life.) Cherubim are humanlike in appearance and are guardians of God's glory. In Muslim lore, the Cherubim were formed from Michael's tears over the sins of the Faithful. They are alluded to as celestial attendants in the Revelation (chapters 4-6). The Prince of the Cherub Choir is Gabriel.

• The **Thrones** represent God's divine justice. Dionysius wrote, "It is through the Thrones that God brings His justice upon us." This third choir is known as the "many-eyed ones" because, when viewed by humans, they are covered with eyes. They are known for their humility and submission to God's will. They reside in the area of the cosmos where material form begins to take shape. The lower choirs of angels need the Thrones in order to access God. The Prince of the Thrones is Orifiel, the angel of Saturday and the planet Saturn. He is also Chief of Talismans.

• The **Dominions** are considered the "Angels of Leadership." Dionysius writes that theirs is the position of authority, regulating the duties of the angels and making known the commands of God. "Through them the majesty of God is manifested." The Prince of the Dominions is Zadkiel, angel of the fourth emanation of Mercy and Lovingkindness.

• The **Virtues** are known as the "Spirits of Motion" and control the elements. Some refer to them as "the shining ones." They govern Nature. They have control over the seasons, stars, moon, and sun. They are also in charge of and perform miracles, and provide courage, grace, and valor. The fifth choir of angels acts on the orders of the Dominions and represents the power of God. The Prince of the Choir of Virtues is Uzziel, one of the principal angels in rabbinic angelology. According to the Book of the Angel (Raziel), Uzziel is among the seven angels who stand before the throne of Glory.

• The **Powers** are warrior angels who fight against evil and defend the heavens and earth. They fight against evil spirits who attempt to bring chaos into the harmony of life. The Prince of this choir is Kamael (Camael). In Druid mythology, Kamael is the Angel of War.

• The **Principalities** is the seventh choir in the hierarchy of angels. Surprisingly, they have hostility toward God and, not so surprisingly, toward humans owing to sin, which is disharmony and imbalance in the Cosmos. The chaos that has come from sin has made them upset and harsh in their judgment. The disciple Paul writes that Christ has gained ultimate rule over them by virtue of his sacrifice in conquering sin and death. (Romans 8:38; 1 Corinthians 15:24; Ephesians 1:21, 3:10, 6:12; Colossians 1:16, 2:10, 15) According to Milton in Paradise Lost (VI, p. 447), the Prince of the Choir of Principalities is Nisroch ("the great eagle"), considered by some to be a demon, continuing the idea that the Principalities are hostile. Of course, some of these descriptions reflect both human and fallen angel fear of the angelic forces.

• **Archangels** are the predominant type of angels mentioned in the Bible and are considered to be the "chief angels" (Jude 9; 1 Thessalonians 4:16). The Archangels are God's messengers to the people at critical times. (Tobit 12:6, 15; John 5:4; Revelation 12:7) The Prince of the Archangels is none other than Metatron.

• The ninth choir is the **Choir of Angels**, which includes our guardian angels, who stand before the throne of God and present our petitions while also watching over us, less we stumble on our way to reunion with our Creator. The Prince of this choir is Phaleg, or Phalec, the governing spirit of Mars, often referred to as the War Lord. Phaleg's signet is among the amulets and talismans of protection (which we will cover later).

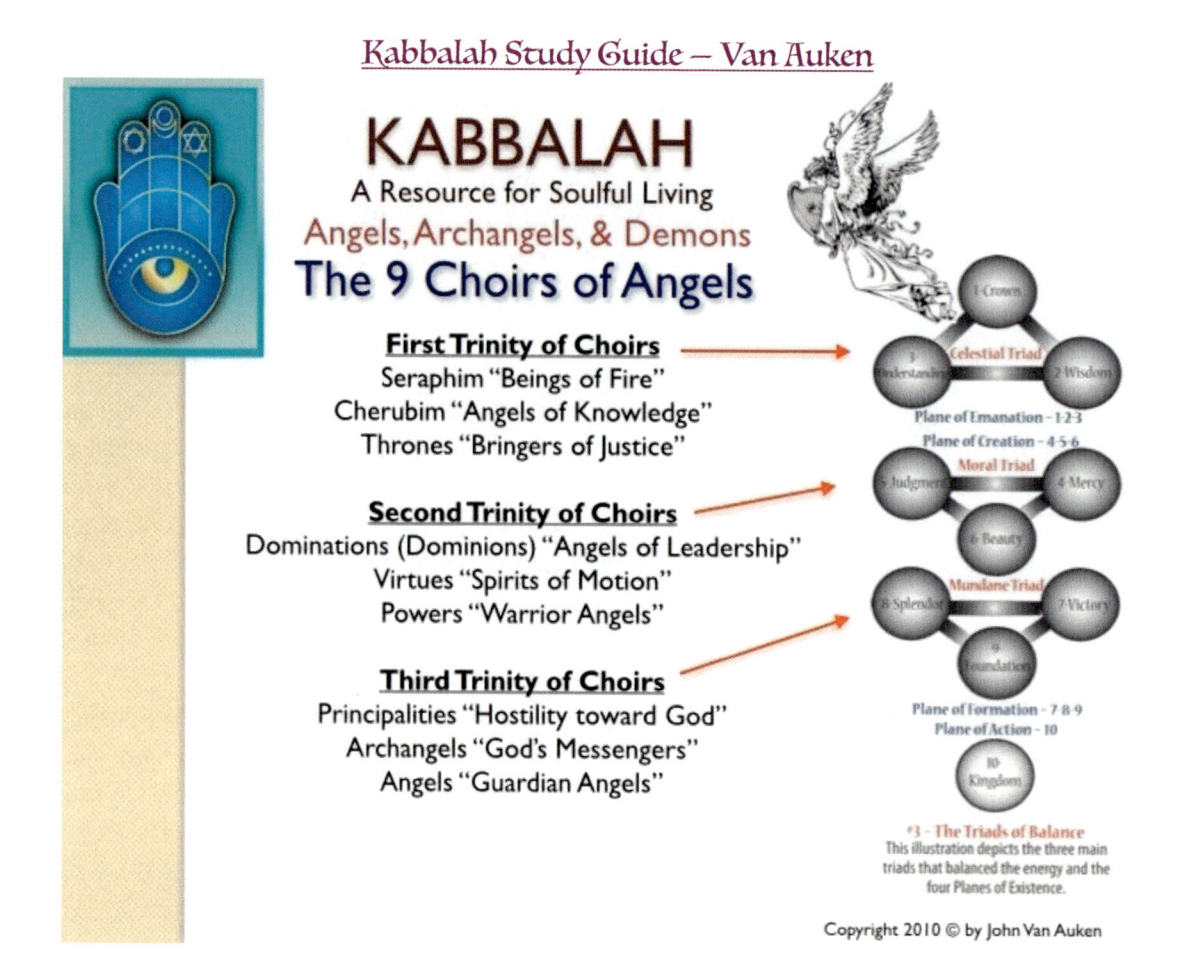

KABBALAH
A Resource for Soulful Living
Angels, Archangels, & Demons
The 9 Choirs of Angels

First Trinity of Choirs
Seraphim "Beings of Fire"
Cherubim "Angels of Knowledge"
Thrones "Bringers of Justice"

Second Trinity of Choirs
Dominations (Dominions) "Angels of Leadership"
Virtues "Spirits of Motion"
Powers "Warrior Angels"

Third Trinity of Choirs
Principalities "Hostility toward God"
Archangels "God's Messengers"
Angels "Guardian Angels"

Plane of Emanation – 1-2-3
Plane of Creation – 4-5-6
Plane of Formation – 7-8-9
Plane of Action – 10

1-Crown, 2-Wisdom, 3-Understanding — Celestial Triad
5-Judgment, 4-Mercy, 6-Beauty — Moral Triad
8-Splendor, 7-Victory, 9-Foundation — Mundane Triad
10-Kingdom

#3 – The Triads of Balance
This illustration depicts the three main triads that balanced the energy and the four Planes of Existence.

Copyright 2010 © by John Van Auken

No biblical writer wrote as much about angels and their choirs as Paul. In fact, most of the Bible does not mention much about angels until Paul's letters in the New Testament, where we learn of the Principalities and Archangels, and several angels are named. Fortunately, there is so much literature beyond the Bible on angels that volumes could be written about the angels and their choirs. Paul himself writes that before his ministry, he ascended (in his body or out of it, he was not sure) to the third heaven, into Paradise, and learned much of what he would subsequently write about.

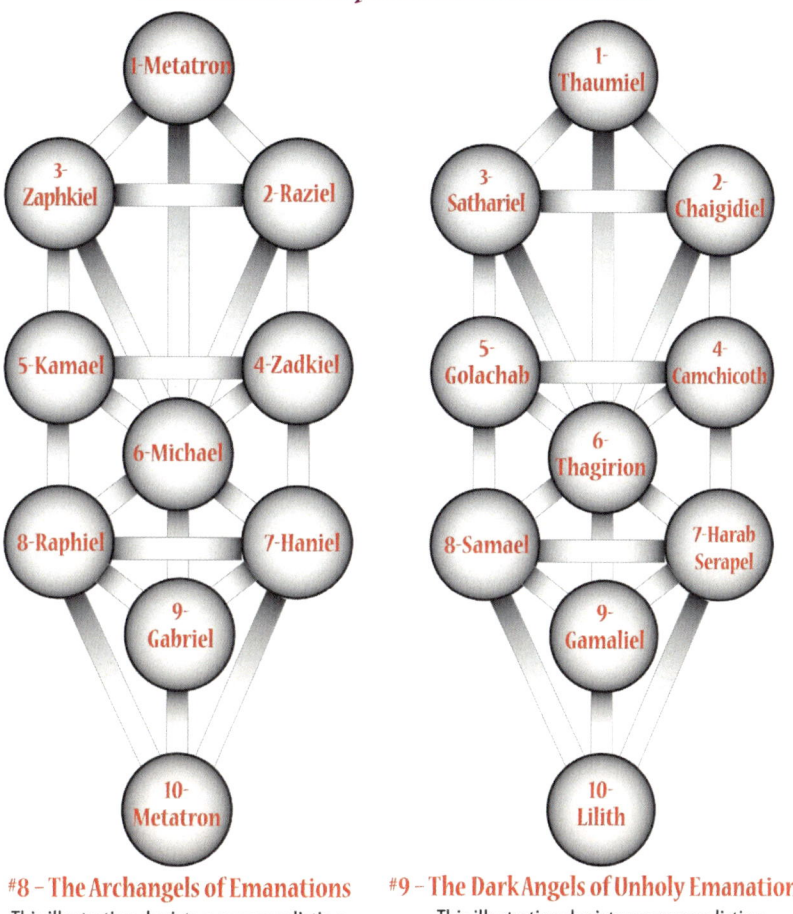

Kabbalah Study Guide – Van Auken

#8 – The Archangels of Emanations
This illustration depicts a common listing the Archangels of each Emanation.

Tree 1 (Archangels):
1-Metatron, 2-Raziel, 3-Zaphkiel, 4-Zadkiel, 5-Kamael, 6-Michael, 7-Haniel, 8-Raphiel, 9-Gabriel, 10-Metatron

#9 – The Dark Angels of Unholy Emanations
This illustration depicts a common listing the Dark Angels of the unholy Emanations.

Tree 2 (Dark Angels):
1-Thaumiel, 2-Chaigidiel, 3-Sathariel, 4-Camchicoth, 5-Golachab, 6-Thagirion, 7-Harab Serapel, 8-Samael, 9-Gamaliel, 10-Lilith

Archangels of the **Emanations** (Sefirot) A **sefira** (singular of sefirot) is an initial emanation of God's holy being during the creation of the universe. As we have studied earlier, there are ten holy and ten unholy sefirot, or shadowsefirot. The holy ones emanated from God's right side, and the unholy from His left. Some writers compare the ten holy sefirot to Plato's powers or intelligences, and with the Gnosticism's "aeons" or "light emanations." As angels, the holy sefirot are arranged in this order (see above illustration): Metatron (crown), Raziel (wisdom), Zaphkiel (understanding), Zadkiel (mercy), Kamael (might), Michael (beauty), Haniel (victory), Raphael (splendor), Gabriel (foundation), and Metatron (kingdom). Notice that Metatron is both the first and the last in this listing, which echoes Paul's writing of the first Adam and the last Adam: "The first man Adam became a living soul. The last Adam became a life-giving spirit." (I Corinthians 15:45) [Note: In some classical Kabbalah schools, Michael is Splendor and Raphael is Beauty, which does seem to fit better with the meaning of their respective names and roles.]

Archangels of the Emanations (Sefirot)

- **Metatron** (crown and kingdom) is called King of the Angels, Angel of the Covenant, Prince of the Presence, and the Lesser Yahweh (the tetragammaton, which is YHWH, the name of the

65

Almighty Father in Heaven). Many believe this name reveals his role as the Logos, God's primary expression into the creation. As the "Logos", the "Word," Metatron is the bridge between humanity and divinity. He is identified with Mercury, Hermes, Enoch, and several other key figures, all of which Cayce's readings identify as incarnations of the Logos, the Messiah. There is even a Kabbalistic connection between Adam and Metatron, a connection that Cayce's readings also make. Kabbalah holds that Metatron was the guiding angel of Israel during the forty-year exodus in the wilderness searching for the Promised Land. The origin of his nonangel-like name is unknown, and it is unusual among Hebrew names. Though difficult to give meaning to some believe the name comes from the Latin *metator*, meaning "a measurer," which would certainly fit with Hermes, who measured the weight of every soul's heart to see if their heart was light enough to enter the heavens, and then recorded the finding in the Scroll, or Book of Life. Metatron maintains "the Archives of Metatron." In Jewish angelology, it was Metatron who stayed the hand of Abraham, keeping him from sacrificing his son Isaac. Metatron resides in the 7th Heaven, the dwelling place of God. When evoked, he appears as a column of fire, his face as bright as the Sun. In the *Zohar*, he is "the rod of Moses," from which comes life from one side and death from the other. Amazingly, Metatron is the Angel of Death while, at the same time, the Angel of Resurrection! The *Zohar* equates him with Adam before he sinned: pure, powerful, and always in the company of God. Curiously, Metatron is also considered to be the teacher of children in Paradise who died prematurely.

- Raziel (wisdom) is the legendary author of Kabbalah's "The Book of the Angel" (Sefer Raziel). His name means "Secret of God." It is said that Noah learned how to build the ark by reading Raziel's tome. Raziel is the Herald of Deity and Preceptor Angel of Adam. According to legend, Raziel's great power is magic. In Targum Ecclesiastes (10, 20), the earliest commentary on the biblical Ecclesiastes, Raziel is the angel that was standing on Mount Horeb proclaiming the secrets to all humanity. In Kabbalah, he is the Chief of the Erelim. The Erelim are the Angels of Peace and are known to weep over destruction and death.

- Zaphkiel (understanding) is the governor of the planet realm of Saturn. His name means "Knowledge of God." He is Chief of the Order of Thrones and Ruler of the Order of Cherubim—the angels sent to guard the gates of Eden. Originally they were depicted as the bearers of God's Throne, as the charioteers, and as powerful beings with four wings and four faces. Zaphkiel is also the Herald of Hell, bringing messages to those that have become lost and suffer in their sins.

- Zadkiel (mercy) is the Angel of Benevolence, Mercy, and Memory, and the Chief of the Order of Dominations. His name means "Righteousness of God." He is ruler of the planet realm of Jupiter. In The *Zohar*, Zadkiel joins with Zophiel (another name for Zaphkiel) when the archangel Michael goes to battle. In some lore and magical books, Zadkiel is the Regent of Hell, ruling over lost souls and sinners—as such, it is comforting to know that he is also the Angel of Mercy.

- Kamael, often Camael, (strength), meaning "He Who Sees God," is the Chief of the Order of Powers. The Druids considered him the god of war. Naturally, he is the angelic guardian of the planetary realm of Mars (the Roman god of war). He is referred to as "the talisman of the angels"; thus the word cameo comes from this angel's name, Camael.

- **Michael** (beauty, or some say splendor) is the Chief of Archangels, Protector of the Presence (of God), and Chief of the Order of Virtues. He is the Angel of Repentance, Righteousness, Mercy, and Sanctification. His name means "Who is as God." He rules the 4th Heaven and is the guardian angel of Israel (all seekers). He is conqueror of Satan (see 12th chapter of the Revelation). His secret name is Sabbathiel (Lord of the Sabbath, "the intermission"), indicating that when humans rest from their willful doing and when they seek God as opposed to their interests, he protects them.
- **Haniel** (victory) means Grace of God, Glory of God, or "He Who Sees God." He is Chief of the Order of Principalities and governor of Venus, as was the Chaldean angel Ishtar. His powers were often evoked by an amulet. His name has been found on many unearthed amulets.
- **Raphael** (splendor, or some say beauty) means "God has Healed." He is one of the presences with powers over diseases and wounds that afflict the children of men. He is one of the three angels that Abraham questioned about saving Sodom and Gomorrah (Genesis 18; the other two were believed to be Michael and Gabriel). Legend holds that Raphael handed Noah a book of healing after he landed and was to begin repopulating the world. He is the Angel of the Sun, Prince of the 2nd Heaven, Chief of the Virtues, Guardian of the Tree of Life, and the Angel of Healing. He is credited as the angel who troubled the healing waters at Bethesda (John 5). This water healed the first to step in it. Raphael is mentioned in The Book of Tobit (a book of the Old Testament Apocrypha.
- **Gabriel** (foundation) means "God is My Strength." In the three religions of "The Book" (Bible)—Judaism, Christianity, and Islam—he is one of the top two angels along with Michael. He and Michael are the only two angels named directly in the Old Testament (other angels are secretly known but not named). Cayce's readings state that "Gabriel is, to be sure, the Announcer." Gabriel presides over Paradise and is the ruler of the 1st Heaven. Mohammed said Gabriel (Jibril, in Islam) dictated the Koran to him. Gabriel is the Guardian Angel of the Ismaelites (the Arabs). He is the angel who appeared to the prophet Daniel and told him all about the future of his people, and was the first to announce the coming of the Messiah. Legend holds that Gabriel was the man-angel that Jacob wrestled with to gain his blessing and new name, Israel. (Genesis 32:24)
- **Metatron** (kingdom) means the "lesser Yahweh," ruler of the first emanation, who also rules this tenth and final emanation. Recall, this is the only emanation that was able to contain God's initial expression of creative explosion of light, life, and consciousness.

Fallen Angels and Demons

There is a distinction to be made between fallen angels and demons. The fallen angels are those who rebelled against God, and were driven out of heaven. Strictly speaking, demons are destructive spirits, and they can possess people and animals, even in some lore they can possess the forces of Nature, as indicated in the statement, "an ill wind blows." Demons were considered to be "unclean spirits." Spirits is the key word here. In this case, spirits are not beings but dispositions, attitudes, and impulses that inhabit beings. They are demonic motivations. And they bring sickness to the healthy, weakness to the strong, foulness to the clean, smuttiness to the upright. Cayce's readings teach that there is a very thin line between the sublime and ridiculous, and demonic spirits often push souls over that line when despite the best of intentions they fall into dark thoughts and actions. All demonic spirits are earthbound and temporary, but all angels, even the fallen ones, are immortal. Yet, they are currently restricted from entering the Gates of Heaven. Keep this in mind as we study fallen angels. In the Dead Sea Scrolls of the Essenes we find prayers intended to "defend the sons of light from the forces of darkness within the cosmic conflict in which they were locked". (García, Martínez Florentino. The Dead Sea Scrolls Translated: The Qumran Texts in English. Leiden: E.J. Brill, 1994.)

In what may be a helpful insight, Cayce identifies the "**Antichrist**" as a spirit rather than a being, a spirit that can possess the best of us and even whole nations! Here's that quote: "Q: In what form does the anti-Christ come, spoken of in Revelation? A: In the spirit of that opposed to the spirit of truth. The fruits of the spirit of the Christ are love, joy, obedience, long-suffering, brotherly love, kindness. Against such there is no law. The spirit of hate, the anti-Christ, is contention strife, fault-finding, lovers of self, lovers of praise. Those are the anti-Christ, and take possession of groups, masses, and show themselves even in the lives of men." (281-16) And in another helpful reading Cayce stated: "Oft - as may be demonstrated in individualities - there are those who are geniuses an yet are so very close to the border that an emotional shock may make a demon of a genius. There are those activities in which a spiritualized cell, by environment, may make of the demon a saint." (281-63) It is the spirit by which a person is moved in feelings, thoughts, and actions that affects their condition. And one may shift their spirit with the slightest of shifts in their heart, in their mind—moving from demon to saint or saint to demon.

At some point in the heavenly activities of the angels, a **rebellion** occurred. It was led by one of the most beautiful angels, **Lucifer**, whose Hebrew name means "light bearer," or "light bringer," and is associated with the morning or day star, Venus. "How art thou fallen from heaven, O day-star, son of the morning!" (Isaiah 14:12) As we read in the biblical Revelation, the rebellious angels were engaged by the archangel Michael and his angelic army, who drove them out of heaven, causing them to fall from their original grace. They were cast into the earth with their leader, Satan, the name given to now fallen Lucifer. (Revelation 12) These are now known as the Angels of Darkness, which include: **Lucifer** (Light Giver), **Ariel** (once of the Choir of Virtues), **Beelzebub** (once of the choir of cherubim, whose name means "Lord of the Flies"), **Belial** (mentioned 178 times in the Edgar Cayce readings and is considered by many to be a form of Satan, formerly an angel of the Choir of Virtues), **Leviathan** (once of the Choir of Seraphim), **Procell** (once of the Choir of Powers), **Raum** (once of the Choir of Thrones), **Semyaza** (formerly of the Choir of Seraphim), **Vual** (formerly of the Choir of Powers), and **Azazel** (once of the Order of Cherubim). During one of his readings, in which he was vulnerable to dark forces, Cayce actually had to struggle to shield himself from the dark angel Azazel. It began when a questioner asked the deeply attuned Cayce to actually contact Azul (one of Azazel's names, which include the variants Azael, Hazazel, and Azrael, meaning "God strengthens"). This dark angel is one of the chiefs of the Fallen Angels. Legend holds that Azazel taught men how to fashion swords and shields, and women how to beautify their eyelids and wear ornaments to entice men to unclean thoughts of sin. He is known as the Rider of the Serpent, Seducer of Men, and Satan's standard bearer. He refused to bow his head before God's newly created Adam—recall that humankind was made lower than the angels but with the potential to judge them. (I Corinthians 6:3 and Hebrews 2:6-7)

Angels of the Dark Side, the "Shells" (Kellipot) Here is the list of the dark angels that came from the dark side with an explanation of their names. These unholy emanations (sefirot) are shadows of the Holy Emanations (Sefirot) and come out of the left side of God.

- **Thaumiel, the "Twins of God," the "Two-Headed" (doubled-mindedness, wanting both God and mammon).**
- **Chaigidiel, the "Confusion of God's Power."**
- **Sathariel, the "Concealment of God," who hides the face of Mercy.**
- **Camchicoth, "Devourers" or "Wasters."**
- **Golachab, Golab, and Usiel, the "Destroyers."**
- **Thagirion, the "Builders of Ugliness."**
- **Harab Serapel, (considered to be plural) means the "Ravens of Death, the leaders of the infernal regions.**
- **Samael, "Desolation."**
- **Gamaliel, "Pollution."**
- **Lilith, the feminine half of the first Adam, giving Adam one hundred children every day, according to Rabbi Eliezer in The Book of Adam and Eve.**

The *Zohar* describes Lilith as "a hot fiery female who at first cohabited with man," but when Eve was created, she "flew to the cities of the sea coast," where she is "still trying to ensnare mankind." In Hebrew writings, the name Lilith first appears in the Alphabet of Ben Sira (circa 900s), though images exist of her that date back to Assyria's golden age. Many rabbis consider her to have been the temptress of Adam and the mother of Cain. Lilith is the shadow of none other than Metatron! However, the Light Feminine consciousness associated with the tenth emanation is Shekinah, known as the "Divine Indwelling" is the ultimate "Bride of the Lord." Gnosticism helps us understand this, identifying the female spirit (*he kato Sophia*) who, in her ideal essence, is the "Lightsome Mother" (*he Meter he Photeine*). In her lower state, however, she is the "Lustful One" (*he Prouneikos*), a once virginal goddess who fell from her original purity. Here we can see both her light and shadow side as well as her ultimate perfection and redemption. All demons are mortal, but in The *Zohar*, Lilith is an immortal until the Messianic Day—a day that is prophesied in Isaiah 37:31: "And the remnant that is escaped of the house of Judah shall again take root downward, and bear fruit upward."

Edgar Cayce's readings identify Lilith as the first Eve and the divine half of the Logos incarnate. Cayce states that Lilith, as the fallen and then redeemed Divine Feminine, was perfected through many incarnations. And Cayce teaches that Eve also had many following incarnations, eventually becoming none other than Mary, the mother of Jesus, to whom the archangel Gabriel gave the famed address: "Hail, thou that art highly favored, the Lord is with thee; blessed art thou among women. Fear not, Mary, for thou hast found favor with God. And, behold, thou shalt conceive in thy womb, and bring forth a son, and shalt call his name Jesus. He shall be great, and shall be called the Son of the Highest, and the Angels Lord God shall give unto him the throne of his father David. And he shall reign over the house of Jacob forever; and of his kingdom there shall be no end." Then said Mary unto the angel, "How shall this be, seeing I know not a man?" And the angel answered and said unto her,

"The Holy Spirit shall come upon thee, and the power of the Most High shall overshadow thee; therefore also that holy thing which shall be born of thee shall be called the Son of God. And, behold, thy cousin Elizabeth, she hath also conceived a son in her old age, and this is the sixth month with her, who was called barren. For with God nothing shall be impossible." —Luke 1:30-37 Clearly, the angel spoke to this woman as a rare and special soul with a major role to play.

This story has all the elements of the Gnostic legend of the Lonesome Mother (Eve) and the Lustful One (Lilith), redeemed in Sophia, the Wise Female. Redemption and resurrection is a path that all may choose to journey, even Lucifer, as reflected in Scripture. Lucifer, under his moniker "Morning Star," is prophesied to rise again and rejoin the heavenly hosts: "I am the Alpha and the Omega, the first and the last, the beginning and the end. Blessed are they that wash their robes, that they may have the right to come to the Tree of Life, and may enter in by the gates into the city." —Revelation 22:13-14 "I am the root and the offspring of David, the bright, the morning star. And the Spirit and the bride say, 'Come.' And he that hears, let him say, 'Come.' And he that is athirst, let him come. He that will, let him take the water of life freely." —Revelation 22: 13-14, 16-17 Seen in these lines are the "root" of David, which was fallen, and the offspring of David, which has risen and become redeemed and restored.

Edgar Cayce on Angels

"(Q) Is the guardian angel a healing force for physical betterment?

"(A) The guardian angel—that is the companion of each soul as it enters into a material experience—is ever an influence for the keeping of that attunement between the creative energies or forces of the soul-entity and health, life, light and immortality. Thus, to be sure, it is a portion of that influence for healing forces.

"And as may be experienced in the activities of individuals, it may become so accentuated as to be the greater influence in their experience. Thus it is as has been given of old: that to some there is the gift of healing, to some the gift of speech, interpreting of tongues, to ministering. Yet all are of the same Spirit. For these are ever that which is the assurance, in that as has been given—God hath not willed that any soul should perish but hath with every temptation, with every condition prepared an association, an activity, a manner, a way for the regeneration of those influences or forces that may cause the overcoming of fear or any of those things that would separate a soul from the Creative Forces.

"Hence, as has been indicated for this body here, the making of the physical adjustments is necessary; but it is just as necessary for the activities of the associations through which the energies of the bodily forces may be attuned to the spiritual and mental self—through the closer association and walk with creative energies within self.

"For all must coordinate. Just as in the Godhead—Father, Son, Holy Spirit—so within self: Body, Mind, Soul. Mind is the Builder; Mind is the Way—as the Christ-Consciousness. As it is directed then through the influences of the bodily functions it becomes aware of its oneness, and thus is the guardian force made to be at-one with the whole of the purposes and desires, and the will of the individual.

"Do these things then, as we find, as indicated, and we will bring to the physical forces a better cooperation and coordination; and thus through the mental application of the at-onement with the Creative Forces, better reactions in every manner.

"(Q) Is it through the guardian angel that God speaks to the individual?

"(A) Ever through that influence or force as He has given, "Ye abide in me and I in thee, as the Father abides in me, so may we make our abode with thee."

"Then as the guardian influence or angel is ever before the face of the Father, through same may that influence ever speak—but only by the command of or attunement to that which is thy ideal.

"What then is thy ideal? In whom have ye believed, as well as in what have ye believed? Is that in which thou hast believed able to keep ever before thee that thou commits unto Him?

"Yes—through thy angel, **through thy self that is the angel**—does the self speak with thy Ideal!" (EC 1646-1)

Notice this last line, because it reinforces the teaching that we are of Divine origin and, despite our present physical condition, we remain connected to our Creator through an unseen portion of our being that is angelic: "through thyself that is the angel."

Notice also that Cayce ties the angelic portion of our being to our ideal. Again and again Cayce's readings ask us, "What is your ideal?" In what and in whom do you believe? Is it our ideal to be among the children of God or simply the children of men? Do we have room in our hearts and minds for heavenly things? Or is it earthly things that matter most to us? You would not be reading this book if earthly things were all that interested you, so let's assume that you are interested in heavenly things and that these have a place in your ideal life and consciousness.

Cayce reveals that our angel is always in communion with God: "The face of self's own angel is ever before the Throne. Commune oft with Him." (EC 1917-1) Jesus affirms this in Matthew's gospel: "Take heed that you despise not one of these little ones [the children gathered around him]; for I say to you, that in heaven their angels do always behold the face of my Father which is in heaven." (Matthew 18:10)

When Edgar Cayce was in the deep trance state through which he obtained readings, his subconscious, or soul mind, could attune to the very highest sources in the spiritual dimensions. In the well-known Search for God study group readings, the 262 series, there were occasions when the archangel Michael would actually speak through Cayce and give powerful messages. Cayce's discourses called Michael the archangel of change:

"Michael is the Lord of the Way—and in the ways of understanding, of conception, of bringing about those things that make for the changes in the attitudes in physical, mental, or material relationships...[Michael] is the guide through such spiritual relations...." (EC 585-1; italics are mine)

When studied as a whole, the Cayce readings indicate that each of us is a soul that is learning to become companionable to God and to the other created beings (the two great commandments: love God; love others). On the earthly side of the soul is a temporary outer persona we call the personality, often referred to by Cayce as "the body mind." This is what you and I consider to be our real self. On the other side of our soul self is a divine portion of our being that is an angel. It is heavenly, has never left its original place with God, and was made in the image of God. This is the "holy immortal" portion of us, as described in Zoroastrian lore. We have a bodily self, a soul self, and an angelic self. These three have three levels of consciousness: conscious mind, subconscious mind (which Cayce describes to be much larger than we currently understand), and superconscious mind.

Kabbalah Study Guide – Van Auken
SECTION 3 PART 2
Incantations and Talismans

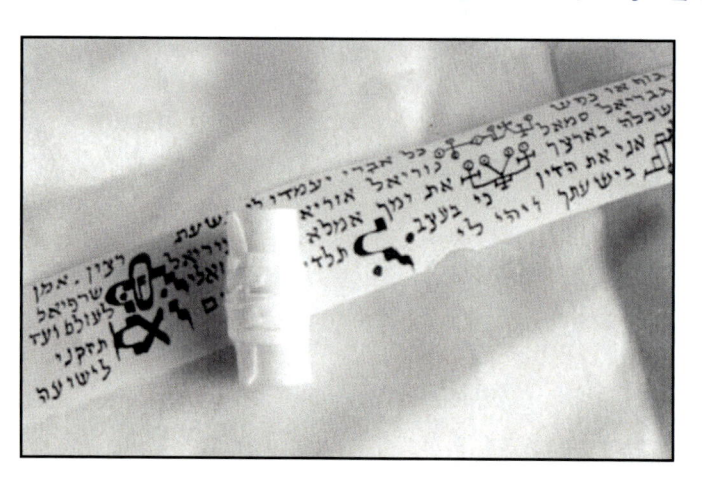

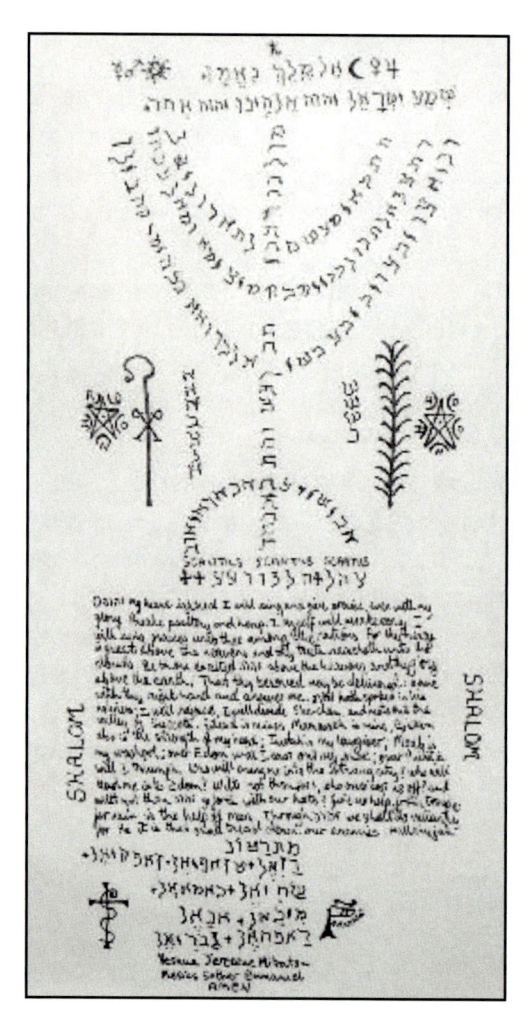

One of the most distinguishing aspects of Kabbalah from traditional Jewish theology is the emphasis on magical power.

This is especially true of the magical power of Hebrew letters and words, particularly the names and attributes of God. However, in the strictest sense, God does not have a name. The numerous names for God in the literature of Kabbalah are descriptive titles for God's various functions and emanations. For example, adonai means "a lord," in this case, the Lord, Adonai. It is a descriptive title rather an actual name.

Kabbalists use the numerical values of the Hebrew letters in words to derive insights into the nature of reality, especially the letters in the various "names" for God, the names of the angels, and significant passages of the Torah. Then they use these secret insights to set up powerful protection and influence in the world of human life, where evil influences have to be countered and opportunities captured.

Talismans

With these secret insights, Kabbalists make talismans (from the Arabic tilasm, ultimately from the Greek telesma, or telein, which means "to initiate"; in this case, into the power to avert evil and evoke good, which are objects intended to protect the wearer and

72

bring good fortune, health, and various other human wants.

Amulets

Talismans can be amulets (from the Latin amuletum, meaning an object that protects a person from trouble) in the form of gems or simple stones, statues, coins, drawings, pendants, rings, plants, certain animals, and even words said in certain situations.

Cameos

A talisman can be a simple cameo. To protect or amend their destiny, individuals would seek the help of a cameo with an image or words with magical power. The name cameo was first mentioned in the Jerusalemite Talmud (tractate of Sabbath, chap.36, par.71). The name indicates a means of connecting the body with an object, such as Tefillin (phylacteries), which are black, leather straps used to connect cubes containing parchment scrolls inscribed with the Shema (daily prayer) and other biblical passages. They are wrapped on the arm and head of men during weekday morning prayers. (The Jewish sect of the Essenes included women in this ritual.)

Anthropologists and archaeologists have found cameos in ancient sites all over the world and have concluded that cameos were used in different cultures as early as the Neolithic period, 9500 BCE.

The Evil Eye

According to anthropologists and archaeologists, most of the cameos from the prehistoric period were designed to protect one from the evil eye (ayin hara). This ancient Western belief (the evil eye is not found in East Asia, with the exception of the Usog curse of the Philippines) is that the evil eye may come directly from the devil, from the devil working through someone, from someone who is envious, or even from someone who mistakenly releases good news or displays good fortune too publicly. There are many instances in both the Tanakh (the Jewish Bible) and the Talmud (rabbinic discussions) of people casting the evil eye. In Europe and America, to ward off a jinx, Ashkenazi Jews exclaim, Keyn aynhoreh! (also spelled Kein ayin hara!), meaning in Yiddish,"No evil eye!"

Attempts to ward off the curse of the evil eye have created many talismans in diverse cultures. As a class, they are called apotropaic (Greek for prophylactic, or protective, meaning "turns away," in the sense that they turn away or turn back the potential harm).

A common talisman is composed of concentric blue and white circles (usually from inside to outside—dark blue, light blue, white, dark blue). This image is considered to be a staring eye that can bend the malicious gaze back to the sorcerer.

A blue eye can also be found on some forms of the hamesh or hamsa hand, an apotropaic hand-shaped amulet against the evil eye found in the Middle East. In Jewish culture, the hamesh is called the Hand of Miriam; in Muslim culture, the hamsa is called the Hand of Fatima.

The evil eye protector, as a visual device, is known to have been common in Greece dating back to at least the sixth century BCE. In Greece, the evil eye is cast away through the process of xematiasma (exorcism), whereby the exorcist silently reads a secret prayer passed over from an older relative of the opposite sex, usually a grandparent. Such prayers are revealed cautiously because there is a superstition that those who reveal them indiscriminately lose their ability to cast away the evil eye.

Kabbalah Study Guide – Van Auken

The Red String Bracelet (Rachel's Bracelet)

Whether it is an ancient custom or a modern commercial product, the red string bracelet has become a special Kabbalah talisman. It comes from a belief that if a red thread is wrapped around Rachel's tomb in Israel seven times while reciting specific Hebrew prayers, especially including Psalm 33, then the wearers of the bracelets made from this thread will carry with them a special blessing, for Rachel loves her children and God loves Rachel. Rachel Emeinu (Our Mother) is considered to be a potent spiritual influence for those in this world.

The bracelet is worn on the left wrist. Judaism.com explains that, "the left heart is full of blood and is home to the Nefesh, the vitalizing animal soul in a person. Wearing the string around the left hand reminds the person of the 'battle' that must be waged against one's selfish urges. "Further," every morning, 'a thread of grace prevails' and G-d renews the world for another day. The string symbolizes that 'thread of grace.'" (Note: Such Jewish writers use "G-d" for "God," rather than write the name completely, because they believe that the name should not be spoken aloud or written.)

One of the prayers said as the red string is being blessed is the Ana B'Koach Prayer. Here is that prayer:

> We implore You by the great power of Your right hand, release the captive.
> Accept the prayer of Your people; strengthen us, purify us, Awesome One.
> Mighty One, we beseech You, guard as the apple of the eye those who seek Your Oneness.
> Bless them, cleanse them; bestow upon them forever Your merciful righteousness.
> Powerful, Holy One, in our abounding goodness, guide Your congregation.
> Only and Exalted One, turn to Your people who are mindful of Your holiness.
> Accept our supplication and hear our cry, You who know secret thoughts.

This mystical poem in Hebrew consists of seven lines with six words per line. The total of forty-two words corresponds to one of the Holy Names of God. The initial Hebrew letters of each word also refer to this Holy Name.

Icons of Protection and Well-being

This very practical side of Kabbalism used magicians known as Ba'alei ha-Shem, or "Masters of the Name," to create deflective charms. They combined the techniques of magic they had acquired from the Babylonians and Egyptians with the authority and power of the holy Hebrew names of God to create a unique form of Kabbalistic magic.

The most famous cameo in history was the Egyptian scarab (beetle), which was an emblem dedicated to Ra, god of the Sun. According to the ancient Egyptians, the dung beetle was a symbol for resurrection from the dung of the world. According to Kabbalah, the beetle was a symbol of infinity. Cayce identifies the scarab with one of the seven ages of humanity in the earth. Like the scarab, the Egyptian ankh was a sacred cameo representing the power of Eternal Life.

In Christianity, the crucifix and the simpler cross are considered to be protective cameos.

Since the Middle Ages, Kabbalah has been the inspiration for creating cameos containing angel's names or names related to God. Kabbalists had a profound influence on Christian mystics, who learned from the Kabbalists how to use the icons.

Incantations

One of the main devices in Kabbalah magic was the audible citing of biblical passages, God's titles, angels' names, and holy names, sometimes in the form of a prayer or actually calling or evoking the divine influence into action on one's behalf. They contained within them "seed sounds," or hidden syllables, which, when spoken aloud, would evoke, or conjure, magical forces. Here again the Kabbalistic idea that God and His forces enter this world through sounds, phrases, and names gives support to this means of channeling power. Most of these were spoken with authority, not begging or beseeching, but commanding. The incantation would often be structured in such a way as to affirm the facts of God's power and presence and the powers of all the forces of heaven. Nothing was left to doubt or uncertainty. Here is an example:

> I, [your name], servant of God, desire, and call upon thee, and conjure thee, Pureness (Tehor), by all the holy angels and archangels, by the holy Michael, the holy Gabriel, Raphael, Uriel, Thronus, Dominations, Principalities, Virtues, Cherubim, and Seraphim, and with unceasing voice I cry, 'Holy, holy, holy is the Lord God of Hosts,' and by the most terrible words: Soab, Sother, Emmanuel, Hdon, Amathon, Mathay, Adonai, Eel, Eli, Eloy, Zoag, Dios, Anath, Tafa, Uabo, Tetragammonaton (YWHW), Aglay, Josua, Jonas, Calpie, Calphas, Appear before me, [your name], in a mild and human form, and do what I desire.

Repetitions of an incantation were required to total one of the magic numbers—3 and 7, occasionally 9—but a caution was given concerning the number 9 because, in some cases, it evoked certain demons and was considered the number of karma. However, among some groups, 9 was and remains a most powerful number. Even so, to repeat an incantation the wrong number of times could also render it useless.

In the following incantation, the repetitions vary and need to be recited precisely to gain the full power of the incantation.

> By Thy universal name of grace and favor Yahweh (but not spoken aloud), set Thy grace Yahweh (again, not spoken aloud) upon [your name], son of [your mother's name], as it rested upon Joseph, the righteous one, as it is said, 'And the Lord was with Joseph, and showed kindness unto him, and gave him favor' in the sight of all those who beheld him [Gen. 39:21]. In the name of Michael, Gabriel, Raphael, Uriel, Kabshiel, Yah [repeat eight times], Ehyeh, Ahah [repeat four times], Yehu [repeat nine times].

When an incantation was being used to undo something, it would often be said backward (which could be a real challenge) or in a diminishing manner. For example, the demon that brought on fever was Ochnotinos. To break his hold on a person, the healing cantor would chant solemnly and with power in his voice: Ochnotinos, chnotinos, notinos, otinos, tinos, inos, nos, os. In this way he would diminish the demon's power until it vanished. When sending one's child off to school, one would incant the name Armimas, the angel of the Sabbath, in a diminishing manner because it was time to stop resting, as was done on the Sabbath, and to start working: Armimas, rmimas, mimas, imas, mas, as.

These incantations were often spoken while also stepping backwards or throwing something over one's back. Other actions were also considered to help the incantation, such as spitting, because human saliva was considered to have magical powers. This idea goes way back to the Maya and ancient Egyptians. Isis received her amazing powers from the spittle of Ra, and the Mayan Mother god made the perfect Blue Maze people from the spittle of the Children of God mixed with the ashes of their mistakes.

Reversing the diminishing chant could also be used to build up a power. One of the best examples is the famous Key of Solomon (Clavicula Salomonis): ton, ramaton, gramaton, ragramaton, tragramaton, and it concludes triumphantly, tetragrammaton (YWHW, Yaweh). This was believed to build up to a point of evoking the very presence of the invisible God and all His forces.

Sometimes these incantations were spoken while standing in a circle or even in concentric circles. There was a belief that demons could not trespass from public territory to private, so standing in one's own circle, one's own space, had protective power that could not be violated. The magician's circle was often scribed with a sword or knife, and sometimes the directions require three or seven concentric circles, the type of metal and the number of circles adding to the protective virtues of this magical method. Often salt was used to form the circle or circles. Interestingly, in the Orient, the general practice at a funeral is for the mourners to circle the coffin seven times, reciting an anti-demon phrase. Similarly the late custom among East-European Jews was for the bride to walk around her groom under the wedding canopy three or seven times – intended to keep off the demons who were waiting to disturb their joy and peace.

Handwritten Cameos and Amulets

Cameos are based on "virtue writing" (the term virtue is being used in its Kabbalistic sense of an energy operating without material or sensible substance—an invisible influence emanating into human life). These writings contain ancient scripts, "angel writing," and King Solomon seals. The cameos that appeared later in history were considered to give powers or problem-solving attributes to those who carried them.

Most handwritten Kabbalah cameos contain verses from the Torah, angel's names, God's names, and Hebrew letters, taken from the person's name requesting the cameo as well as the mother's name. In Jewish magic, the sacred name of a person includes the mother's name, and the same rule appears in Greek and Arab magic. In post-Talmudic Aramaic incantations and in the medieval texts, it was quite consistently adhered to, the father's name occurring only rarely. This practice comes from Menahem Recanati's explanation of the *Zohar*. "All magic comes from woman." In Psalm 116:16, it is clearly stated that every man is "the son of thy handmaid." This follows the secret sin of Adam that we considered in the week on emanations: Adam caused the Divine Feminine, who is the handmaid of God, to become divorced from her heavenly mate. As humankind allows the feminine to reunite with the heavenly, humankind then regains magical power.

In the Middle Ages, Kabbalists created amulets according to instructions received during séances and channeling sessions. These cameos were written combinations of letters and symbols and would evoke, or conjure, magical forces.

Here are three examples of written charms:

Adonai Sabaoth ("Lord of Hosts," "Lord of Armies"), give grace, love, success, charm to the bearer of this amulet.

Ehyeh Asher Ehyeh ("I Am Who I Am"), ha-nora ha-gibbor ("the mighty one," "the hero").

Ehyeh Asher Ehyeh ("I Am Who I Am"), hayei olam le-olam ("eternal life forever").

Early in Jewish history, as a way to save space on precious and scarce writing materials (easy-to-produce paper was centuries away), Jewish scribes developed an elaborate list of abbreviations for commonly used phrases and terms. For example, the title for God, Ha-Kadosh Barukh Hu ("The Holy Blessed One"), became HKB"H. Such acronyms were known as Roshei Teivot, meaning the "heads of words," and these cover the pages of traditional Jewish works such as the Midrash. Here are some samples of acronyms found on written virtues:

- ShYCh"G—Shuvah Yah Chatzah Nafshi—"Return O Eternal, save my life." (from Psalm 6:5).

Here's one with simply a title for God:
- Sh"Y—Shomer Yisrael—"Guardian of Israel." (from Psalm 121).

Acronyms can also convey a verse from a Jewish prayer, as in this example:
- AGL"A—Atah Gibor L'olam Adonai—"You are Forever Powerful, O Eternal."

(This is the Gevurot prayer, the second blessing of the "18 Blessings," Shemoneh Esrei.)

Here are two solemn appeals:
- BACh"V—Bashem El Chai V'kayyam—"[Do this] in the name of the living and enduring God."
- BM"T—B'Mazal Tov—"[bless me] with good fortune."

Here's a call for the protection of angels:
- ARGM"N—Uriel, Rafael, Gabriel, Michael, Nuriel.

Another might contain the sum of ten emanatons of Kabbalah's sefirot, as in this last example:
- CHBT"M—Chochmah, Binah, Tiferet, Malchut— translated these name mean: "Wisdom, Understanding, Beauty, Kingdom."

King Solomon Seals

King Solomon Seals are the most powerful symbols in Judaism and Christianity. Each symbol carries its special attributes of power.

According to practical Kabbalah, the King Solomon Seals are famous for their tremendous powers and are used widely for amulet writing.

The secret of writing amulets properly is in the hands of a few masters who know how to write a faultless and complete seal. A specific script is used for each person's individual request. The text is written in ancient Hebrew scripts and angel writing on a special kosher (legal) parchment, made of deer skin (also used for Mezuzah scrolls), using feather and ink. It is well developed and written according to the name, the birth date, and the mother's name of the person ordering it, and fitted to solve the problem or the request.

The most effective handwritten amulets, apparently, are those dedicated to the requester personally and prepared as just mentioned.

Magic in the Psalms

The Medieval Jewish text Shimmush Tehillim ("On the Use of Psalms") probably formed the basis for Godfrey Selig's (1673-1708) Secrets of the Psalms: A Fragment of the Practical Kabbalah. Each of these books explains how to use words and phrases from the Psalms. Here are some examples from The Sixth and Seventh Books of Moses by Johann Scheible and Moses and Joseph Ennemoser. The accompanying comments are those of Eoghan Ballard of the University of Pennsylvania:

Psalms for Making Peace between Husband and Wife

Psalms 45 and 46—Whoever has a scolding wife, let him pronounce the 45th Psalm over pure olive oil, and anoint his body with it, then his wife, in the future will be more lovable and friendly. But if a man has innocently incurred the enmity of his wife, and desires a proper return of conjugal love and peace, let him pray the 46th Psalm over olive oil, and anoint his wife thoroughly with it, and, it is said, married love will again return.

Eoghan Ballard: Psalm 45 refers to anointing with "the oil of gladness" and to the "rejoicing" that occurs when the "glorious" daughter of the King of Tyre is brought before the King. Psalm 46 contains the words, "God is in the midst of her...God shall help her...He makes wars to cease unto the end of the Earth."

Psalm to Make Your Home Lucky

Psalm 61—When you are about to take possession of a new dwelling, repeat this Psalm just before moving in, with a suitable prayer, trusting in the name of Schaddei ("the True God"), and you will experience blessing and good fortune.

Eoghan Ballard: Psalm 61 contains the lines, "Thou hast been a shelter for me, and a strong tower from the enemy. I will abide in Thy tabernacle forever; I will trust in the covert of Thy wings." Psalm for Safe Travel at Night Psalm 121—When you are compelled to travel alone by night, pray this Psalm reverently seven times, and you will be safe from all accidents and evil occurrences. Eoghan Ballard: Psalm 121 opens with the line, "I will lift up mine eyes unto the hills, from whence cometh my help." Psalm for Severe Headache or Backache Psalm 3—Whosoever is subject to severe headache and backache, let him pray this Psalm [...] over a small quantity of olive oil, [and] anoint the head or back while in prayer. This will afford immediate relief.

Eoghan Ballard: Psalm 3 contains the line, "Thou, O Lord, art a shield for me; my glory, and the lifter of mine head."

Psalm for a Repentant Liar

Psalm 132—If you have sworn to perform anything punctually, and notwithstanding your oath you neglect to perform your obligation, and in this manner have perjured yourself, you should, in order to avoid a future crime of a similar kind, pray this Psalm daily with profound reverence.

Eoghan Ballard: Psalm 132 contains the line, "The Lord hath sworn the truth unto David; he will not turn from it."

The 10 Words of Creation

The following is a powerful magic built on the first lines in the Bible. Naturally, they are called The Ten Blessings of Creation (Asser Ma'Amarot) and correspond to the ten emanations (sephirot):

1. Genesis 1:3— "Let there be light," and there was light.
2. Genesis 1:6— "Let there be an expanse in the midst of the waters, and let it divide the waters from the waters."
3. Genesis 1:9— "Let the waters under the sky be gathered together to one place, and let the dry land appear," and it was so.
4. Genesis 1:11— "Let the earth put forth grass, herbs yielding seed, and fruit trees bearing fruit after their kind, with its seed in it, on the earth," and it was so.
5. Genesis 1:14— "Let there be lights in the expanse of sky to divide the day from the night; and let them be for signs, and for seasons, and for days and years."
6. Genesis 1:20— "Let the waters swarm with swarms of living creatures, and let birds fly above the earth in the open expanse of sky."
7. Genesis 1:24— "Let the earth bring forth living creatures after their kind, cattle, creeping things, and animals of the earth after their kind," and it was so.
8. Genesis 1:26— "Let us make man in our image, after our likeness: and let them have dominion over the fish of the sea, and over the birds of the sky, and over the cattle, and over all the earth, and over every creeping thing that creeps on the earth."

9. Genesis 1:28— Blessed them, "Be fruitful, multiply, fill the earth, and subdue it. Have dominion over the fish of the sea, over the birds of the sky, and over every living thing that moves on the earth."
10. Genesis 1:29— "Behold, I have given you every herb yielding seed, which is on the surface of all the earth, and every tree, which bears fruit yielding seed. It will be your food."

SECTION 3 PART 3

Kabbalah and the Meaning and Magic of Numbers

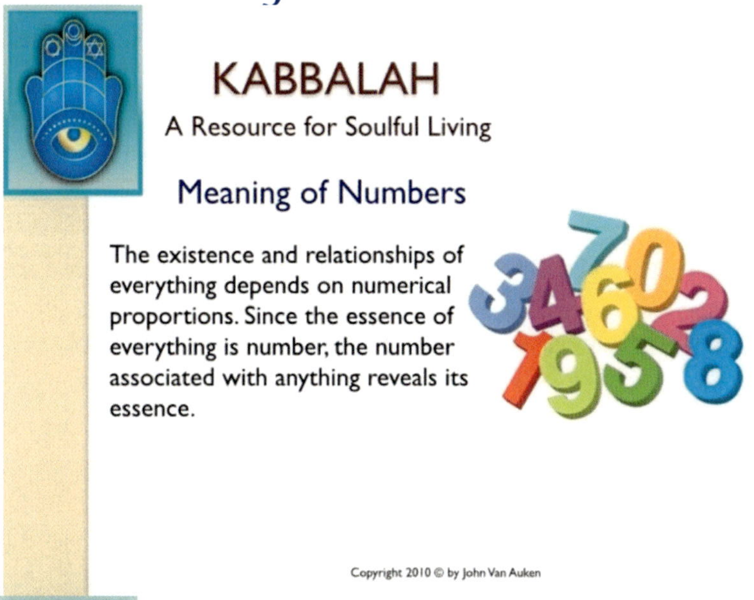

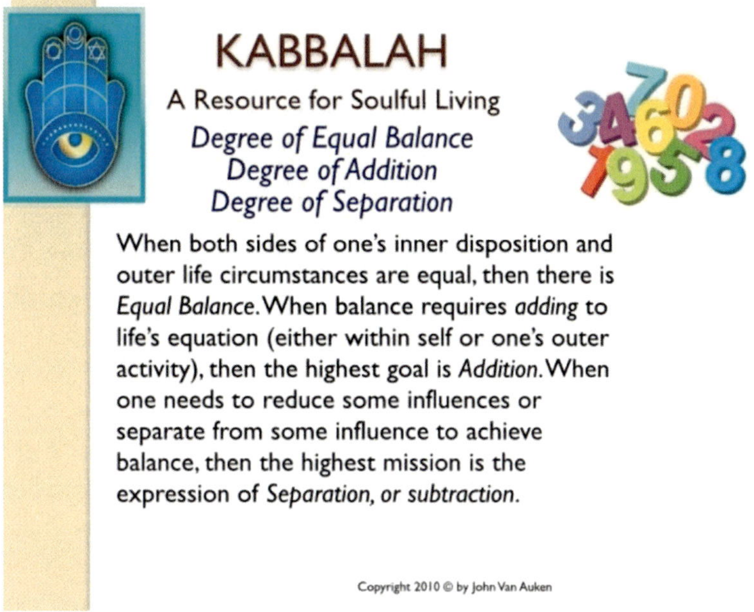

KABBALAH
A Resource for Soulful Living

Meaning of Numbers

The existence and relationships of everything depends on numerical proportions. Since the essence of everything is number, the number associated with anything reveals its essence.

Copyright 2010 © by John Van Auken

KABBALAH
A Resource for Soulful Living

Degree of Equal Balance
Degree of Addition
Degree of Separation

When both sides of one's inner disposition and outer life circumstances are equal, then there is *Equal Balance*. When balance requires *adding* to life's equation (either within self or one's outer activity), then the highest goal is *Addition*. When one needs to reduce some influences or separate from some influence to achieve balance, then the highest mission is the expression of *Separation*, or subtraction.

Copyright 2010 © by John Van Auken

The translation of the Hebrew word sefirah is "counting," although it has many connotations, our focus having been on its use as an emanation. For the Kabbalists, each number rules manifestations that fit that number. Seven, for example, rules the seven orifices in the human head (eyes, ears, nostrils, and mouth), the seven days of the week, the seven planets of ancient astrology, the seven chakras, and so on. Four is found in the "city four square" and the four elements of this world, and the like. Twelve rules the Zodiac, months, and so on.

"The Book of Creation" (Sefer Yezira), more scientific than religious, indicates that the creation, at one level, was accomplished by divine speech. Hinduism also presents the idea that sound created the universe. There are twenty-two letters in the Hebrew alphabet, and there are 231 possible variations using these twenty-two letters. Rabbi Harav Yitzchak Ginsburgh writes that "two-letter units are sub-roots, each sub-root being a gateway to meaning and understanding. We are taught in Kabbalah that there are 231 gates." The Hebrew word for gate (sha'ar) also means "opening," and it is through these openings that the Word of God expressed the Creation. Each of these numbers is a creative portion of the ensemble of the Creation.

Kabbalah teaches that all of creation emanated from the Ein Sof, the Infinite Eternal. It did so through the sefirot, the ten emanations of Its being expressed in the Tree of Life. From the tenth emanation came the twenty-two letters of the Hebrew alphabet. These letters are more than letters; they are powers with numerical values. From these numerical powers the whole finite universe came into existence. Number is the essence of all things. The existence and relationships of everything depends on numerical proportions. Since the essence of everything is number, the number associated with anything reveals its essence.

All the twenty-two letters are coordinate powers. Even so, the number 3 is obviously different from the number 6, and computations of numbers will differ according to the components involved. But it is important to keep in mind that all is one, and each expression contains a portion of the Whole.

Allow me for a moment to be a bit abstract in an attempt to reveal how numbers may be adjusted to achieve harmony and balance. In Kabbalah, there are three levels of high numerical expression: Equal Balance, Addition, and Separation. When both one's inner disposition and outer life circumstances are equal, then there is Equal Balance. When balance requires adding to life's equation (either in self or in one's outer activity), then the highest goal is Addition. When one needs to reduce some influences or separate from some influence to achieve balance, then the highest mission is the expression of Separation. Each mission has its degree, hence the designations Degree of Equal Balance, Degree of Addition, and Degree of Separation, respectively. When examining oneself and one's life, it is helpful to consider these three principles and the degree of need to find ultimate harmony.

Kabbalah numerology gives numeric values only to letters, words, and names, whereas traditional numerologies commonly evaluate dates and numbers as well.

Kabbalah numerology can become so complicated as to confuse and distract from one's soul journey, leaving one lost in the multiplicity of this dimension. For example, in one system the numerical value of a letter is "filled" (*miluim*), or expanded. Using this method, the letters in the name of God become words with sums of 72, 63, 45, and 52, but each letter has variant spellings, so there are 27 possible expansions of the Holy Name. When all of this is calculated, the expansion totals 1521! Even so, God is Oneness. We are not going through this maze to get to the simple truth that God is one.

In this chapter we will focus only on the primary numerical values and their helpfulness to our soul growth. The Kabbalah numerology used here is based on key chapters in The Book of Creation (*Sepher Yetzirah*). It is expressed in the ten emanations and the twenty-two channels through which the energy of the Tree of Life flows.

Numbers are all around us, of course: the date we were born, our address, our phone numbers, social security numbers, our automobile tags, and our name all have numbers associated with them. Every day, month, and year has a number associated with it. Cayce advises us to approach numerology in a much different manner than commonly practiced today. The numbers do not dictate our conditions or opportunities, they reflect the conditions or circumstances within which we determine, by the use of our free will, what will be built. If we keep this in mind, we will get the most out of numbers and numerology.

We build for ourselves certain situations, rhythms, patterns, habits, and surroundings—in a "normal" day's cycle, in a week's cycle, in a year's cycle—that naturally influence our demeanor. We can take this to mean that our disposition and temperament change naturally as the movement of the cycles stimulate us in different ways, but we determine how we react or use them.

Think of it this way: what are you like at 6 a.m.? What are you like at 6 p.m.? What are you like and what are the influences in your life in winter months? In summer months?

We have to take responsibility for our role in the numbers around us and know that we have the innate power to change our reaction to any condition by using our God-given free will. Even when circumstances are blowing against us, we can always tack against that wind, like a good sailor, until we reach a more favorable breeze as the cycle shifts again. We are the key to what the numbers mean and how we use the influences they represent.

Number 1

From a Kabbalistic perspective, the number 1 represents both the beginning and the oneness within which multiplicity exists. One is first, and all the numbers follow from the one.

The first expression reflects the Infinite Eternal's creativity, which is motivated and guided by love. Here are the Creative Forces, as opposed to the destructive ones. Here is the womb of Divine Love that conceived the entire Universe—and cares. The first emanation of the Divine on the Tree of Life is the "I AM that I am."

Some Kabbalists believe this first emanation of God reveals the Creator's concern for Its creation, having the sole purpose of shielding the world and the world's beings from the brilliant yet blinding light of the Creator, thus it is the

"Concealed Consciousness." In ancient Egypt this would be Amon Ra (or Amun Ra), the so-called hidden aspect of God.

In the number 1 is the entire plan. It is wholeness. The entire creation exists within the 1. Diversity and multiplicity exist within the oneness of the whole.

One is also centeredness. A heart and mind that is centered is a place of tranquility and clarity in a sea of activity. In centeredness it calls for an ideal. The ideal creates a principle around which all activity proceeds purposefully, orderly, and balanced. As images of the Divinity, we need our plan, or ideal, from which our growth and direction are guided.

The weakness of 1 is stagnation. Thus, the number 2 becomes necessary, for it is a channel through which we implement the plan, the ideal.

Kabbalah Study Guide – Van Auken

Number 2

From a Kabbalistic perspective, the number 2 reflects a consciousness stimulated to execute the plan of life and enlightenment. Two is a readiness to express, a willingness to go forth and make manifest the plan. This motivation and momentum is the father of all created things. In 1 the plan is conceived; in 2 is the impetus to carry out the plan.

The number 2 reflects the second emanation of the Infinite Eternal: Wisdom (Chokhmah). The 2 looks up to the I AM to perceive the plan, and then seeks to implement what it perceives.

A soul with the number two desires to express, to go forth and assist life to flow according to the Divine Plan. In 2 we find a search for Wisdom, a love for Wisdom—but especially wisdom expressed or applied in life and in relationships.

The number 2 is considered masculine and has the attributes of the father. It is the archetype of fatherhood, for it is referred to as the "Father of Fathers," and it is within this context that 2 is mystically synonymous with Eden. Eden was a key aspect of the initial plan. It was a prototype, a model. The ideal world was revealed in the initial ensample, Eden.

Kabbalistically, 2 is the "Wisdom-Gushing Fountain," the "Water of the Wise," and is called the "Illuminating Consciousness" because it takes what it gleans from Concealed Consciousness and expresses it.

The weakness of 2 is division, which may create a sense of "otherness." Even numbers, as opposed to odd numbers, have traditionally been considered the weaker numbers, because they can be divided; thus, they are not stable. The I AM and Wisdom need the triad strength of Understanding to become stable. The number 2 is a wise eye, but it needs the eye of understanding to gain depth of perception. This leads to the number 3.

Number 3

From a Kabbalistic perspective, the number 3 is Understanding. It is the Cosmic Mother (Imma), within whose womb all that was contained in the number 1 and perceived by the number 2 finally becomes distinguished, clarified, and comprehendible. This emanation is considered the Mother of Mothers. It is feminine. In the blending of mother Understanding with father Wisdom a conception occurs, giving life to the next seven emanations on the Tree of Life.

According to the Kabbalistic symbolism of the Palace, or Divine Mansion, the appearance of the number 3 represents the unfolding of what was once hidden but is now knowable. The stage that was Wisdom (number 2) now expands through the nourishing that comes from Understanding. She is called the "Sanctifying Consciousness," for she takes the Concealed and the Illuminating and prepares them for the next stages of Creation while shielding them from potential contamination and confusion.

The coming seven days of Genesis will flow out of her womb, birthing the next seven emanations.

In Gnostic teachings, the number 3 is the key to all mysteries. The three supreme principles are (1) not-created, (2) self-created, and (3) created. The Ideal has a threefold nature, threefold body, and threefold power. Of course, the triangle has three sides, and in the diagram of the universe—a triangle within a circle—it represents the triune condition within the infinite whole.

Body, mind, and soul comprise the triad of our being. Physical, mental, and spiritual are the dynamics of our reality. If one aspect is greater than another, the balance is lost.

Three's weakness is that, in distinguishing the parts from the whole, it becomes distracted by the parts and thereby loses sight of the oneness of all life. The 3 also has the weakness of imbalance, resulting in struggles and inequities. Balance must be maintained. For example, a three-legged stool is not a sound foundation. It tips over very easily unless the weight it maintains is centered. Likewise, with balance maintained, 3 has the strength of the triad, which is a stabilizing dynamic in the Tree of Life.

Number 4

From a Kabbalistic perspective, the number 4 reflects the fourth emanation of the Tree of Life, that of the Loving Kindness and Mercy of God (Chesed). The number 4 is considered a masculine force, the productive "doer" power, which manifests itself in the universe and in humanity. It is said that the powers of Love and Mercy contained in the number 4 were so great that the aspects of the number 5 had to be created to set a limit on the all-merciful, all-loving flow in order to sustain truth and order!

Kabbalah teaches that this orb on the Tree of Life represents the first day of Creation in Genesis. On this day God created light and separated the darkness from that light to make the first day and night. In the beginning God created the heavens and the earth. And the earth was waste and void; and darkness was upon the face of the deep; and the Spirit of God moved upon the face of the waters. And God said, 'Let there be light,' and there was light. And God saw the light, that it was good; and God divided the light from the darkness. And God called the light Day, and the darkness he called Night. And there was evening and there was morning, one day. Genesis 1:1-5

The number 4's awareness is called "That Consciousness Which Receives and Contains." It is given this title because it contains the spiritual emanations of the Higher Consciousness of the Creative Spirit expressed out of the union of the Triad of the I AM, father Wisdom, and mother Understanding.

Its weakness is in division, separation, and scatteredness, losing its centeredness amid multiplicity. It becomes too lovingly outpouring of its life force while unable to retain its vital connection to Infinite Energy. It must maintain its receptive container characteristic—balancing the Light from above with the need from below.

Number 5

From a Kabbalistic perspective, the number 5 represents an awareness called "Radical Consciousness," because it is closest in equality to the Supreme Crown (number 1) and emanates from the depths of Wisdom.

The number 5 represents the fifth aspect, or emanation, of the Tree of Life, the Judgment and Might of God (Gevurah). Its nature is feminine, and it limits the abundance of Love and Mercy (number 4) to hold to truth and order. By the same token, the severities of Power in the 5 are tempered by the Love and Mercy of 4, so the two exist in a state of harmonic balance on the Tree of Life.

This aspect of the Tree of Life is symbolically the second day of Genesis when God separated the waters by creating a firmament. And God said, "Let there be a firmament in the midst of the waters, and let it divide the waters from the waters." And God made the firmament, and divided the waters that were under the firmament from the waters that were above the firmament; and it was so. And God called the firmament Heaven. And there was evening and there was morning, a second day. Genesis 1:6-8 The firmament symbolizes a truth, a place upon which one establishes his or her ideals and guiding standards. Now the waters above are separated from the waters below.

The number 5 is also discernment, the power to see through muddled situations and thoughts, separating good from evil, right from wrong, true from false. This is why Kabbalism considers 5 to be "Truth Consciousness."

The weakness of 5 is cold-heartedness, as when judgment slips into condemnation, and love and mercy have no longer any offsetting balance to the power of 5.

Number 6

From a Kabbalistic perspective, the number 6 represents the awareness called "Consciousness of the Mediating Influence." Six seeks to resolve discordant influences. Six is cooperation, holistic vision, and the bridging of opposites. It mediates the extremes, bringing them to balance.

The number 6 also refers to the sixth aspect of the Tree of Life, Beauty and Balance (Tiferet). It is a beauty through balance and harmony, through health and liveliness.

This number has an androgynous form, meaning it contains both male and female aspects. The source of this androgyny has its origin between the Creator's two arms, that part which expands from the heart to all parts of the whole. This portion of the Tree of Life gives life to art, music, and creativity.

The sixth emanation represents the third day of Genesis, when the waters under heaven were gathered in one place and the dry land appeared. It was the day when grass and herbs and fruit trees were created. And God said, "Let the waters under the heavens be gathered together unto one place, and let the dry land appear"; and it was so. And God called the dry land Earth; and the gathering together of the waters he called Seas:and God saw that it was good. And God said,"Let the earth put forth grass,herbs yielding seed, and fruit-trees bearing fruit after their kind, wherein is the seed thereof, upon the earth"; and it was so. And the earth brought forth grass,herbs yielding seed after their kind,and trees bearing fruit,wherein is the seed thereof, after their kind; and God saw that it was good. And there was evening and there was morning, a third day. Genesis 1:9-13

Even though 6 is an even number, and even numbers are categorized as the weaker numbers, 6 is considered to have no weakness.

Number 7

From a Kabbalistic perspective, the number 7 represents the awareness called "Mystical Consciousness," because its virtues are hidden and only seen by the eyes of the spiritually minded. This stage of the path awakens the connection to one's true relationship as an active member of humanity, nature, and the cosmos. Along this path, one realizes and actualizes one's true potential.

The number 7 also refers to the seventh aspect of the Tree of Life,Victory and Fortitude (Netsah). It is a masculine, active principle that achieves victory through endurance. It has an intuitive sense of individuality in the midst of universality. It is infinite in the midst of the finite reality.

This aspect of the Tree of Life symbolically represents the fourth day of Genesis, the day on which God created the lights in the heavens as signs. Seven sees the meaning in signs, symbols, and the passage of time. And God said, "Let there be lights in the firmament of heaven to divide the day from the night; and let them be for signs, and for seasons, and for days and years; and let them be for lights in the firmament of heaven to give light upon the earth";and it was so. And God made the two great lights;the greater light to rule the day, and the lesser light to rule the night: he made the stars also. And God set them in the firmament of heaven to give light upon the earth, and to rule over the day and over the night, and to divide the light from the darkness; and God saw that it was good. And there was evening and there was morning, a fourth day. Genesis 1:14-19

Seven awakens to the hidden meaning of life as it is revealed through illumination and revelation. Seven is a life and a consciousness of victory over all that hinders the soul in its journey.

The weakness that may manifest in the number 7 is excessive otherworldliness, which results in losing a sense of the purposefulness of this incarnation, with its circumstances and relationships. One's head may be in the higher heavens, but one's feet must be firmly planted on the ground of this reality and its opportunities.

Number 8

From a Kabbalistic perspective, the number 8 represents the awareness called the "Perfecting Consciousness." It is from here that the ability to prepare principles to live by emanates. Eight attaches itself to the roots hidden in the depths of Love and Mercy (Chesed, number 4) and then springs forth with principles to live by.

The number 8 is Splendor and Glory (Hod). Once the inertia of doubt, uncertainty, and fear is overcome and the drive toward enlightenment vitalized, the soul can be filled with the spirit of healing and resurrection. This transformation is symbolized by the splendor of God that fills the mind and heart. Eight may become a light to all.

This number symbolizes the fifth day of Genesis during which God created the creatures of the sea and air. And God said, "Let the waters bring forth swarms of living creatures, and let birds fly above the earth in the open firmament of heaven." And God created the great sea-monsters, and every living creature that moves, wherewith the waters swarmed, after their kind, and every winged bird after its kind; and God saw that it was good. And God blessed them, saying,

"Be fruitful, and multiply, and fill the waters in the seas, and let birds multiply on the earth." And there was evening and there was morning, a fifth day. Genesis 1:20-23

Eight realizes its full potential through perfecting its consciousness. It is fruitful, creative, and multiplies through daily living of what it knows is best, as revealed by God's splendor and glory flowing through all life.

Eight fills physicality, materiality, and the world with the light and wisdom of the heavens and God's goodness. In 8, the physical and the spiritual find harmony and balance. In 8, physical life finds spiritual purpose and meaning. For 8s, relationships become opportunities to apply the "fruits of the spirit"—love, kindness, patience, understanding, gentleness, and forgiveness.

The weakness of 8 is that its joy for this world can become so materialistic as to diminish space in the mind and heart for spiritual, ethereal awarenesses and activities.

Number 9

From a Kabbalistic perspective, the number 9 represents the awareness called the "Purifying Consciousness," because it purifies the numbers, qualifies and adjusts the manner in which they are represented, and unites them so that they may not suffer division and destruction.

The number 9 also refers to the ninth aspect of the Tree of Life, the Foundation and Bonding (Yesod). Upon the foundation of 9, all aspects of the Tree of Life achieve their ideal.

Nine is the élan vital, the life force, the kundalini energy. Nine has a sexual quality to it, not in the sense of sexual activity but in the nature of the two genders and Creation. In 9 the two genders are bonded in harmony, bringing forth a new birth, a new consciousness. Nine is symbolic of both the male and female root chakra. Nine is the sexual organ of the "Divine Hermaphrodite," God's bonding of Heavenly Father and Mother.

Nine is representative of the sixth day of Genesis, when God created male and female in one (they are not separated until the second chapter of Genesis). And God said, "Let us make man in our image, after our likeness; and let them have dominion over the fish of the sea, and over the birds of the heavens, and over the cattle, and over all the earth, and over every creeping thing that creeps upon the earth." And God created man in his own image, in the image of God created He him; male and female created He them. And God blessed them; and God said unto them, "Be fruitful, and multiply, and replenish the earth, and subdue it; and have dominion over the fish of the sea, and over the birds of the heavens, and over every living thing that moves upon the earth."

And God said, "Behold, I have given you every herb yielding seed, which is upon the face of all the earth, and every tree, in which is the fruit of a tree yielding seed; to you it shall be for food; and to every beast of the earth, and to every bird of the heavens, and to everything that creeps upon the earth, wherein there is life, I have given every green herb for food"; and it was so. And God saw everything that he had made, and, behold, it was very good. And there was evening and there was morning, the sixth day. Genesis 1:26-31

Because the sixth day of Creation is the last day of Creation (God rested on the seventh day), the number 9 represents completion. Nine signifies the finishing of what was begun. The weakness of 9 is in the handling of the stewardship over all of the creatures and creation that God assigned to us. This manifests in no stewardship, poor stewardship, or excessive dominance over the creatures and the creation. And since 9 is considered to be the number of karma, there is a price to pay for abuse of stewardship.

Kabbalah Numbers 11 and 22
Kabbalah 11

From a Kabbalistic perspective, the number 11 represents the eleventh awareness, the "Scintillating Consciousness," so named because it is the garment held up before the "Formations and the Order of the Superior and Inferior Causes," referring to the movement from the Plane of Formation and the Mundane Triad to the Plane of Creation and the Moral Triad. To possess this path is to enjoy great dignity and to come face to face with the Cause of Causes. Such contact is scintillating.

Kabbalah 22

From a Kabbalistic perspective, the number 22 represents the twenty-second awareness, "Consciousness of the Faithful," or "Faithful Consciousness," because it is filled with spiritual virtues, which are increased until their complete enlightenment and luminescence is realized.

Kabbalah Triplets—666 and More

In classical Kabbalism, the number 666 was associated with the persecuting Roman Emperors, most often with Nero, but some associated the number with cruel Domitian. A broader interpretation would be to associate it with Roman power as a symbol of worldly power, as opposed to heavenly—man's power versus God's. Since the number of the beast is required to sell or purchase, this fits well. "No one can buy or sell unless he has the mark, that is, the name of the beast or the number of its name." (Revelation 13:17) It is the number of materialism, commercialism, and mammon. It is also the number of earthly humanity without any awareness of higher purposes and planes.

In a Gnostic illustration with Greek terms and Kabbalah numbers, we find a map of the levels of consciousness and energetics. The source of this image is *Apocalypse Unsealed* by James Morgan Pryse, published in 1910.

Diagram: Four circles labeled Head (points 5, 6, 7), Heart (point 4), Navel (point 3), and Genitals (points 1, 2), connected by a serpentine line. To the right:

1000 *Ho Nikon*, the Conqueror
999 *Epistemon*, Intuitively Wise
888 *Iesous*, the Higher Mind
  I. "The Lamb of God"
777 *Stauros*, the Cross

666 *He Phren*, the Lower Mind
  II. "The Beast"

555 *Epithumia*, Desire
  III. "The Red Dragon"

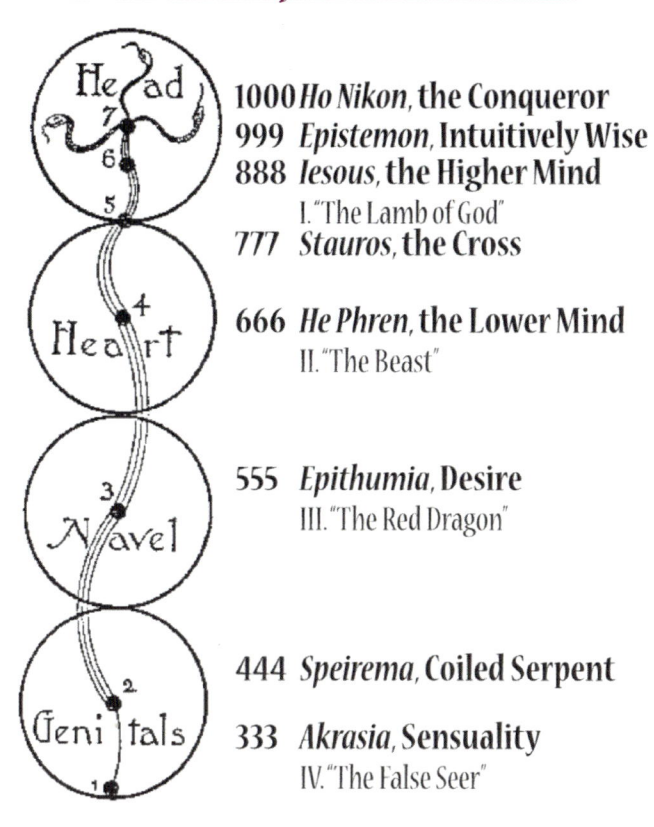

444 *Speirema*, Coiled Serpent
333 *Akrasia*, Sensuality
  IV. "The False Seer"

#26 – Gnostic and Kabbalistic Kundalini

Kabbalah numbers and Gnostic terms correlated to the spiritual centers of the body and the Revelation.

From the bottom we begin, and the journey to resurrection and enlightenment proceeds. (The name for each number is followed by its name in Greek and the Greek meaning of the word.)

333, "The False Seer," Akrasia (lacking command over oneself).
444, "the Serpent-coil," Spirema (coil).
555, "the Red Dragon," Epithumia (desire, craving, longing, desire for what is forbidden, lust).
666, "the Beast," He Phren (the lower mind; parts of the heart and the mind).
777, "the Cross," Stauros (a cross; an upright stake).
888, "the Lamb," Iesous (Jesus, meaning "Jehovah is salvation").
999, "Intuitively Wise," Epistemon (imbued with knowing).
1000, "the Conqueror," Ho Nikon (the victor, conqueror).

In Revelation, when the disciple John sees the number 666, he knows what it symbolizes and why it is called the number of the beast: because it is the lower mind that never seeks higher consciousness and is not willing to endure the sacrifice necessary to reach such higher awareness. That sacrifice is symbolized in the number of the cross—777—upon which one must crucify desire in self that our real potential may be realized.

Kabbalah Study Guide – Van Auken

SECTION 4 PART 1
Ecstasy of God Consciousness

אלהים חיים

"The Living God"

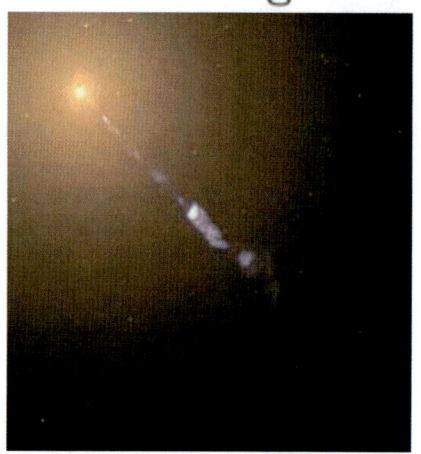

KABBALAH
A Resource for Soulful Living

Ecstasy

The Zohar gives us a wonderful transitional sense of moving from daily consciousness to heavenly consciousness by helping us understand the transition to sleep and even to death, then using the understanding of these natural transitions to generate a movement to higher consciousness using intentional meditative techniques.

Copyright 2010 © by John Van Auken

KABBALAH
A Resource for Soulful Living
Ecstasy

The Zohar also uses the metaphor of marriage between a man and a woman as a model for meditative attunement to God, using sexual terms to generate the ultimate sexual union. This is a classic concept dating back to ancient Asia using yin and yang as model for the union of these dualistic qualities to realize higher states of consciousness and the ecstasy union—reunion.

Plato held that, deep down, eros love actually seeks transcendental beauty, but human beauty reminds one of that transcendent beauty.

Copyright 2010 © by John Van Auken

We cannot fully appreciate Kabbalah without understanding the mystic's experience of direct, personal contact with the Infinite Eternal (Ein Sof) and the ecstasy of such a face-to-face communion with the Divine. Preparing the body, the mind, and the soul for such an encounter is the secret practice of the true Kabbalist.

Abraham Abulafia (1240-1291) of Spain and Italy, whose revelations resulting from his attunement to the Divine nearly got him burned at the stake by Pope Nicholas III. Abulafia wrote a series of manuals describing how to attain mystical ecstasy. Abulafia believed that the Hebrew letters and key words in the Scriptures have secret powers and, when used like mantras, may bring on divine ecstasy. He developed a technique called "the knowledge of the combinations" (hokhmath ha-tseruf), using the infinite combinations of the letters of the Hebrew alphabet and rearrangements of spiritual words to generate an altered state of consciousness with God. He required that these sounds be repeated extensively while music is being played. The result would be spiritual ecstasy.

The Spanish Castilian mystics associated with Jacob ben Jacob ha-Cohen and Isaac ben Jacob ha-Cohen [ben means "son of"] also used Hebrew letters and names for God to magically generate an ecstatic sense of union with God.

The *Zohar* gives us a wonderful transitional sense of moving from daily consciousness to heavenly consciousness by helping us understand the transition to sleep and even to death, then using this understanding of these natural transitions to generate a movement to higher consciousness using meditative techniques. The *Zohar* also uses the metaphor of marriage between a man and a woman as a model for meditative attunement to God, using sexual terms to generate the ultimate sexual union. This is a classical concept dating back to very ancient times in Asia using the terms yin and yang as an explanation of the union of these dualistic qualities to realize higher states of consciousness and the ecstasy that results from oneness. In our case, it is the oneness that results from our intimate merging with the Source of our life, with Elohim, with the Infinite Eternal.

Merkabah mystics use the metaphor of Ezekial's chariots to ride through the heavens. One of the strongest movements of mystical, ecstatic Kabbalistic practices was among the fifteenth- and sixteenth-century mystics of a town called Safed in Asia Minor (modern-day Turkey). Safed concepts and methods spread throughout the eastern Mediterranean—from Turkey to Egypt, including Palestine, and as far away as Persia—and became known asLurianic Kabbalism, titled after its founder Isaac Luria (1534-1572), who was also known as the "Ari "(Hebrew for lion). Lurianic mystics seek that "emptiness" to which God withdrew in order for the Creation to take place (remember this from Week 1)—they seek out that "pure emptiness" (tehiru), which is a common concept in deep meditation practices around the globe in many cultures and mystical schools. I think of it as "the womb of Mother God"—still, silence, but so alive with the essence beneath all expressed life. Once we touch this sacred place, we are never the same again.

Ecstasy, in the sense that we are using the word, was best defined by Plotinus (204–270 BCE, the founder of Neo-Platonism, author of Enneads):

> "The liberation of the mind from its finite consciousness,
> becoming one and identified with the Infinite."

It is this moment from an individual's consciousness to conscious contact with the Universal Consciousness of God that is the mystic's goal and guides his or her methods.

Direct, personal contact with the Divine was what the early Kabbalistic seekers sought. And though they sought it within the context and community of laws, rituals, and traditions, their personal contact with the Divine set them apart from the greater community. Such experiences, and the methods used to have such experiences, became secret because the greater community could not deal with such a personal connection between a human and God. The devil had to have a role in any such divination, and during some of Kabbalah's greatest times of popularity, the Inquisitor was empowered and could sentence such mystics to the fires of the stake, especially if they were not Christian, as was the case with the Kabbalists. This was a dangerous practice in those days, but experiencing God's presence was so worth the danger that many sought to learn and practice these methods.

Even though many rituals, magical practices, and angelic hierarchies—and complexities upon complexities—have been added to the codexes and lore of Kabbalah, it is the ecstasy of direct, personal contact that is at the root and core of Kabbalah. Paradoxically, it is the singular, infinite, unseen God (Ein Sof) within which all these complexities have their being that the mystic makes the ecstatic contact that inspires, rejuvenates, and transforms heart and mind, soul and spirit. These moments strengthen one's faith, nourish one's soul, enliven one's spirit, and give value to the life of the seeker.

Kabbalah teaches that the unseen God is limitless, invisible, inaudible, and even inaccessible—which appears to make it impossible for one to have any contact with the Divine. How, then, can anyone have direct, personal contact with the purest essence of the Divine? The answer requires an understanding of the original Creation. Before Creation, the infinite Creator was "the fullness of being." The Creation was expressed out of the womb of God's consciousness. Multiplicity, diversity, activity, and dimensions upon dimensions were now the fullness of being. Even so, the original condition of the

Divine remained—a mysterious, silent, hidden void within which all expressed life now moved and had its being.

Contacting the Divine in its post-Creation state requires a type of perception that is alien to anything we know in the midst of the active creation. Normal human senses cannot perceive it. Jesus indicated this when he said, "Those who have ears to hear, let them hear what the Spirit says."

In a discussion with Flaccus, a fellow seeker of the Infinite, Plotinus explained:

"You ask, how can we know the Infinite? I answer, not by reason. It is the office of reason to distinguish and define. The Infinite, therefore, cannot be ranked among its objects. You can only apprehend the Infinite by a faculty superior to reason, by entering into a state in which you are your finite self no longer—in which the divine essence is communicated *to you*. This is ecstasy. It is the liberation of your mind from its finite anxieties. Like only can apprehend like; when you thus cease to be finite, you become *one with the Infinite*. In the reduction of your soul to its simplest self, its divine essence, you realize this union—this Identity."

Of note in this statement are three key points: (1) The Infinite cannot be ranked among its objects, its creations; (2) One must enter a state of consciousness in which one is no longer its finite self; and (3) Only like can comprehend like, or as many have written, the Great I AM and the little "I am" greet one another, one being the expression of the other.

Moses asked God for his name, and God replied, "I am that I am." In this mystical answer is the liberation of self and finite consciousness to oneness with the Divine and Infinite Consciousness. The Great I AM put its essence deep into the little "I am." And, as Moses learned by his face-to-face contact with God, the "I AM" is the quintessence latent deep within the little "I am." The little "I am" can therefore contact that place within itself that is a portion of its Creator, and thereby contact the source and sustainer of its life.

Such contact brings communion, renewal, and a peace that passes understanding.

Experiencing our heavenly Mother and Father personally, consciously, is ecstasy. To touch the womb of our genesis, to feel the arms of our divine parents, to walk through the Garden with our Creator is a happiness and contentment that cannot be found in any other activity. We have known these states of consciousness, and we can know them again. Sadly, even when we reconnect with this primordial condition, the world and selfish interests can pull us away again. It takes much training and practice to connect, and then the right heart to maintain the connection – all in the midst of free-willed life and individualness.

At its core, Kabbalah is about the ecstatic union and communion between the created and the Creator.

SECTION 4 PART 2
Spiritualizing Body, Mind, and Soul

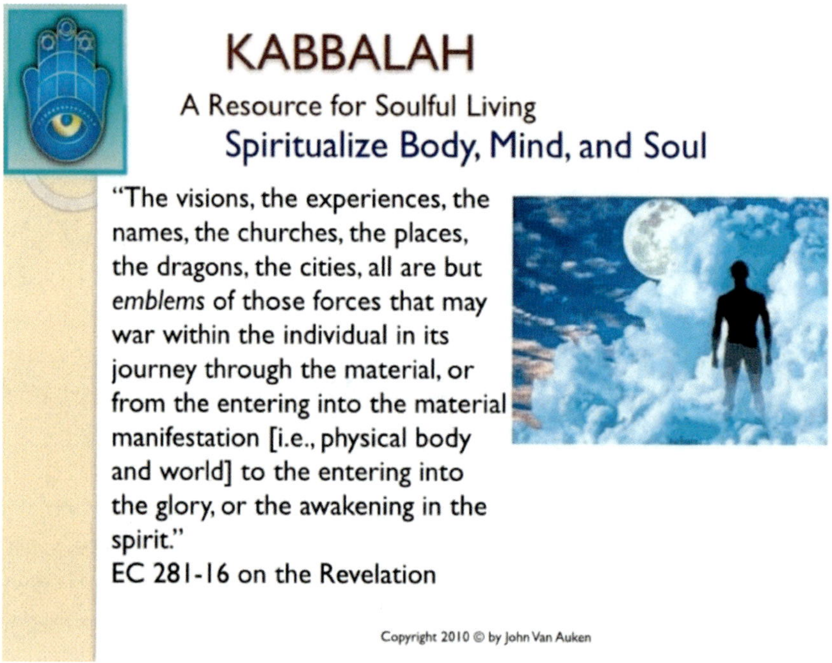

KABBALAH
A Resource for Soulful Living
Spiritualize Body, Mind, and Soul

"The visions, the experiences, the names, the churches, the places, the dragons, the cities, all are but *emblems* of those forces that may war within the individual in its journey through the material, or from the entering into the material manifestation [i.e., physical body and world] to the entering into the glory, or the awakening in the spirit."
EC 281-16 on the Revelation

Copyright 2010 © by John Van Auken

In the journey from Eden to the final chapters of Revelation, there are mystical visions revealing heavenly secrets. If we understand these visions, we will gain insight into how we may become more cosmically conscious, more celestial, more spiritual, and even regain our lost immortality. Let's examine the visions of Isaiah, Elijah, Ezekiel, Daniel, and especially John in his Revelation. And let's do so with an eye toward the messages of soul growth found in the imagery and symbolism of these visions.

But first, let's review one of the biggest biblical tips for communing with God. It is found in a story about Elijah.

Elijah and the Still Small Voice

Here are the passages covering this event:

"The angel of The Lord came again the second time, and touched him [Elijah], and said, 'Arise and eat, because the journey is too great for you.' He arose, and ate and drink, and went in the strength of that food forty days and forty nights to Horeb the Mount of God. He came there to a cave, and lodged there; and, behold, the word of The Lord came to him, and he said to him,'What are you doing here, Elijah?' He said, 'I have been very jealous for The Lord, the God of hosts; for the children of Israel have forsaken your covenant, thrown down your altars, and slain your prophets with the sword: and I, even I only, am left; and they seek my life, to take it away.' He said, 'Go forth, and stand on the mountain before the Lord.' Behold, the Lord passed by, and a great and strong wind tore the mountains, and broke in pieces the rocks before the Lord; but the Lord was not in the wind; and after the wind an earthquake; but the Lord was not in the earthquake; and after the earthquake a fire; but the Lord was not in the fire: and after the fire a still small voice." –I Kings 19:7-12; WEB

In this little story is revealed a great teaching for all who seek communion with God. God does not commune in power and might but in stillness. As the psalm reveals:"Be still, and know that I am God." (Psalm 46:10) Notice also that the voice came from within Elijah, draped in his heavy mantle, standing at the mouth of the cave. In the cave of our deeper consciousness, wrapped in the mantle of protection of our God-seeking heart, keenly seeking communion, the voice of God came to Elizjah and comes to us. That voice was not booming. Rather, it was still and small. How does one hear a still voice? We feel it with our intuition.

For us to commune with the Ein Sof, the Infinite Eternal, we have to learn to sense God's presence within us and hear God's still, small voice. We do not do this with our outer senses. It is achieved, as Elijah's story implies, via an inner, meditative seeking. Cayce taught that it was more "feeling" the presence than hearing or seeing it— and as in telepathy, Cayce said it would come as "a knowing" rather than a sound. As true seekers, we need to develop our skills with meditation and the deep stillness and attunement that is the goal of deep meditation.

With this in mind, let's proceed to the fascinating and revealing visions of the biblical seers upon whom God bestowed wondrous blessings.

Isaiah, Ezekiel, Daniel, and John

As we read these accounts, notice how many similar images, numbers, and characters there are among these visions, even though some may have a different name or title. They reflect a pattern of both God's presence and our connection to God: physically, mentally, and spiritually. Read these as if all the objects and activities are metaphors for inner places and channels of spiritual energy, especially spiritual, cleansing energy. Consider the temple or the house to be our body, and the levels to be both physical and mental, especially levels of consciousness in our deeper mind. Earth would represent our physical consciousness and reality. Angels would be heavenly aspects of ourselves and others at their soul level, while wings would be uplifting energies and thoughts. Covering the face would symbolize reversing outward-looking perception to inward seeking. The wasting of cities and houses would be cleansing the temple of body and mind of the many earthly things, thoughts, and desires.

Isaiah

I saw the Lord sitting on a throne, high and lifted up; and his train filled the temple. Above him stood the seraphim (angels). Each one had six wings. With two he covered his face. With two he covered his feet. With two he flew. One called to another, and said, "Holy, holy, holy, is Lord of Hosts! The whole earth is full of his glory!"The foundations of the thresholds shook at the voice of him who called, and the house was filled with smoke. Then I said, "Woe is me! For I am undone, because I am a man of unclean lips, and I dwell in the midst of a people of unclean lips; for my eyes have seen the King, Lord of Hosts! "Then one of the seraphim flew to me, having a live coal in his hand, which he had taken with the tongs from off the altar. He touched my mouth with it, and said, "Behold, this has touched your lips; and your iniquity is taken away, and your sin forgiven." I heard the Lord's voice, saying, "Whom shall I send, and who will go for us?" Then I said, "Here I am. Send me!" He said, "Go, and tell this people, 'You hear indeed, but don't understand; and you see indeed, but don't perceive.' Make the heart of this people fat; make their ears heavy, and shut their eyes; lest they see with their eyes, and hear with their ears, and understand with their heart, and turn again, and be healed." Then I said, "Lord, how long?" He answered, "Until cities are waste without inhabitant, and houses without man, and the land becomes utterly waste, and the Lord has removed men far away, and the forsaken places are many in the midst of the land. If there are yet a tenth in it, it also shall in turn be eaten up; as a terebinth [a type of tree], and as an oak, whose stock remains, when they are felled; so the holy seed is its stock." –Isaiah 6:1-13

    The trees may have been felled, but within them is their original seed, from which a better tree will grow. This is reminiscent of Jesus' brief but poignant teaching: "Truly, truly, I say to you, unless a grain of wheat falls to the earth and dies, it remains alone; but if it dies, it bears much fruit. He who loves his life loses it, and he who hates his life in this world will keep it for eternal life." (John 12:24-25) This is not to mean that we must physically die to this life and world; rather, we must subdue this reality in order to perceive the more subtle realms of life. It is as William Wordsworth penned not so long ago in his poem "The World is Too Much With Us."

> The world is too much with us; late and soon,
> Getting and spending, we lay waste our powers;
> Little we see in Nature that is ours;
> We have given our hearts away, a sordid boon!
> This Sea that bares her bosom to the moon,
> The winds that will be howling at all hours,
> And are up-gathered now like sleeping flowers,
> For this, for everything, we are out of tune;
> It moves us not. —Great God! I'd rather be
> A Pagan suckled in a creed outworn;
> So might I, standing on this pleasant lea,
> Have glimpses that would make me less forlorn;
> Have sight of Proteus rising from the sea;
> Or hear old Triton blow his wreathed horn.

    Proteus was one of the "first born," as indicated by his Greek name. Triton was "the messenger of the deep," a sea god, son of Poseidon. In the Aeneid, Misenus, brother-in-arms of Hector of Troy and the trumpeter of Aeneas (here representing our earthly self), challenged Triton (here presenting our godly self) to a trumpeting contest. For such arrogance, Triton flung him into the sea.

    Let's take from these images and stories a sense of how we must subdue our earthliness in order to awaken and make room for our spiritual nature and our soul growth. The outer self must grow in humility, meekness, and patience in order for the true, inner self to awaken and resurrect us from our terrestrial paradigm.

Ezekiel

Ezekiel tells us, "The heavens were opened, and I saw visions of God." (Ezekiel 1:1) Again, as we read, let's keep a metaphoric perspective and consider the images and activities to be about forces within our bodies and minds. For example, the beasts in this coming vision symbolize those earthly urges that so often possess our better nature. They symbolize the four lower chakras, or spiritual centers, in our bodies. The firmament dividing the higher realms from the lower ones represents the veil that cloaks, or limits, our consciousness.

Here is an excerpt from one of Ezekiel's visions:

"And there was a voice above the firmament that was over their heads [the heads of the four beasts]: when they stood, they let down their wings. And above the firmament that was over their heads was the likeness of a throne, as the appearance of a sapphire stone; and upon the likeness of the throne was a likeness as the appearance of a man upon it above. And I saw as it were glowing metal, as the appearance of fire within it round about, from the appearance of his loins and upward; and from the appearance of his loins and downward I saw as it were the appearance of fire, and there was brightness round about him. As the appearance of the bow that is in the cloud in the day of rain, so was the appearance of the brightness round about. This was the appearance of the likeness of the glory of the Lord. And when I saw it, I fell upon my face, and I heard a voice of one that spoke. And he said unto me, 'Son of man, stand upon thy feet, and I will speak with thee.' And the Spirit entered into me when he spoke unto me, and set me upon my feet; and I heard him that spoke unto me. And he said unto me, 'Son of man, hear what I say unto thee; be not thou rebellious like that rebellious house; open thy mouth, and eat that which I give thee.' And when I looked, behold, a hand was put forth unto me; and, lo, a roll of a book was there [a scroll]. And he spread it before me; and it was written within and without; and there were written lamentations, and mourning, and woe."

—Ezekiel 1:25-28 and 2:1-10

These lines are so similar to those in the Revelation that we should read them now: I saw a mighty angel coming down out of the sky, clothed with a cloud. A rainbow was on his head. His face was like the sun, and his feet like pillars of fire. He had in his hand a little open book. The voice that I heard from heaven, again speaking with me, said, "Go, take the book which is open in the hand of the angel who stands on the sea and on the land." I went to the angel, telling him to give me the little book. He said to me, "Take it, and eat it up. It will make your stomach bitter, but in your mouth it will be as sweet as honey." I took the little book out of the angel's hand, and ate it up. It was as sweet as honey in my mouth. When I had eaten it, my stomach was made bitter. They told me, "You must prophesy again over many peoples, nations, languages, and kings." Revelation 10:1-2 and 9-11

A brief story about Jesus

Then Jesus was led up by the Spirit into the wilderness to be tempted by the Devil. When he had fasted forty days and forty nights, he was hungry afterward. The tempter came and said to him, "If you are the Son of God, command that these stones become bread." But he answered, "It is written, 'Man shall not live by bread alone, but by every word that proceeds out of the mouth of God.'" –Matthew 4:1-4

In this passage Jesus was referring to the passage in Deuteronomy:

"He humbled you, and allowed you to hunger, and fed you with manna, which you didn't know, neither did your fathers know; that he might make you know that man does not live by bread only, but by everything that proceeds out of the mouth of the Lord does man live." –Deuteronomy 8:3

Daniel

The prophet Daniel describes his encounter this way:

"I lifted up mine eyes, and looked, and, behold, a man clothed in linen, whose loins were girded with pure gold of Uphaz [Ophir]; his body also was like the beryl, and his face as the appearance of lightning, and his eyes as flaming torches, and his arms and his feet like unto burnished brass, and the voice of his words like the voice of a multitude. And I, Daniel, alone saw the vision; for the men that were with me saw not the vision; but a great quaking fell upon them, and they fled to hide themselves. So I was left alone, and saw this great vision, and there remained no strength in me; for my comeliness was turned in me into corruption, and I retained no strength. Yet heard I the voice of his words; and when I heard the voice of his words, then was I fallen into a deep sleep on my face, with my face toward the ground. And, behold, a hand touched me, which set me upon my knees and upon the palms of my hands. And he said unto me, 'O Daniel, thou man greatly beloved, understand the words that I speak unto thee, and stand upright; for unto thee am I now sent.' And when he had spoken this word unto me, I stood trembling. Then said he unto me, 'Fear not, Daniel; for from the first day that thou didst set thy heart to understand, and to humble thyself before thy God, thy words were heard, and I am come for thy words' sake.'" –Daniel 10:6-12

Daniel's description of the messenger from heaven is similar in many ways to that of the disciple John's in the Revelation, which follows.

John

The Gospel writer John has become an icon of Christianity, but he was the son of the Jews Zebedee and Salome and was himself well trained in mystical Judaism, as indicated by his writings. He considered himself to be a "true Jew." His vision that became the Revelation was received and written while he was in banishment to the little island of Patmos off the coast of Asia Minor (Turkey today). He begins his writing by telling us that he was "in the Spirit on the Lord's Day when I saw and heard," and he describes his encounter this way:

"I turned to see the voice that spoke with me. And having turned I saw seven golden candlesticks; and in the midst of the candlesticks one like unto a son of man, clothed with a garment down to the foot, and girt about at the breasts with a golden girdle. And his head and his hair were white as white wool, white as snow; and his eyes were as a flame of fire; and his feet like unto burnished brass, as if it had been refined in a furnace; and his voice as the voice of many waters. And he had in his right hand seven stars, and out of his mouth proceeded a sharp two-edged sword, and his countenance was as the sun shines in his strength. And when I saw him, I fell at his feet as one dead. And he laid his right hand upon me, saying, 'Fear not; I am the first and the last, and the Living One; and I was dead, and behold, I am alive for evermore, and I have the keys of death and of Hades. Write therefore the things which thou saw, and the things which are, and the things which shall come to pass hereafter.'" –Revelation 1:12-19

The book of Daniel is considered the prophecy book of the Old Testament, and the Revelation that of the New Testament. Both authors see a similar messenger from heaven and receive visions of what has been, what is, and what will be. In our study, let's focus on the microcosmic aspects of their message, that part that relates to our personal soul growth.

The messenger figure is the deeper, higher, spiritual, angelic aspect of our whole being. It is that portion made in the image of God and has maintained its proximity to God's throne. To John, this figure says, "Do not be afraid; I am the first and the last, and the Living One; and I was dead, and behold, I am alive forevermore, and I have the keys of death and Hades." As with John, our spiritual self—made in the image of God and destined to be an eternal companion to God—has been dead to us, and will remain so until we give birth to it again, as Jesus instructed Nicodemus: "Verily, verily, I say unto thee, except one be born anew, he cannot see the kingdom of God. You must be born a second time. That which is born of the flesh is flesh; and that which is born of the Spirit is spirit." (John 3:3-6) The first instruction from the spiritual self is to the seven spiritual centers of the body, represented by the various sevens throughout the initial chapters of Revelation.

The idea that the body possesses seven centers, or chakras, which may be used for spiritualization dates back to ancient times. One of the first recorded manuscripts to teach this is Patanjali's Yoga Sutras, written in the ancient Sanskrit language around 300 B.C. Patanjali was a student and teacher of the one of the most ancient texts of religious literature yet found in the world, the Veda, c. 1200 BCE. (The oldest Hebrew text is the Torah, The Book of the Law, dating to 1446 BCE.) Vedism was the religion of an ancient Indo-European people who settled in India. One of Vedism's key teachings, which eventually made its way into another ancient Sanskrit text, the Bhagavad Gita (c. 200 BCE), is that the Supreme Being created our souls with an eternal share of Himself/Herself in each soul, but this share is latent within us and must therefore be awakened. (Bhagavad Gita, XV, 7-11) Cayce affirms this concept when asked, "Should the Christ-Consciousness be described as the awareness within each soul, imprinted in pattern on the mind and waiting to be awakened by the will, of the soul's oneness with God?" and Cayce answered, "Correct. That's the idea exactly!" (EC 5749-14) Patanjali teaches that this latent Presence is in all of creation and, most important to us, in each physical body, able to be awakened by using the physical body in special ways. The body that is so helpful with physical activity secretly contains centers and pathways for metaphysical activity.

To experience this shared Presence of the Supreme Being, Patanjali teaches that one needs to elevate the normal levels of body energy and mental consciousness. The levels we find sufficient for everyday life are not sufficient for intimate contact with God.

In the Vedic texts and most other Eastern texts, energy and consciousness are symbolized by the cobra serpent. We Judeo-Christian followers often equate evil and Satan with the serpent; however, the teachings of Moses and Jesus contain serpent images as part of spiritualization, specifically the raising of the serpent.

During a clandestine nighttime meeting, Nicodemus, a member of the Sanhedrin (the Jewish leadership council), asked Jesus to explain the secret teachings. Jesus gave him three: The first is that we must be born again—we have been born physically, but we need also to be born spiritually. The second is that no one ascends to heaven but he or she who first descended from heaven. All of us, whether we remember it or not, have a portion within us that first descended from heaven. The third teaching uses the serpent to symbolize energy and consciousness: "As Moses raised the serpent in the desert, so must the Son of man be raised up to eternal life." Jesus is referring to the time when Moses left the kingdom of the pharaoh (so symbolic of the outer ego and worldly pursuits) to search for God in the desert. In his search he came upon a deep well around which were seven virgins attempting to water their flocks. These seven maidens symbolize the seven spiritual centers within our body. The deep well in the desert is the biblical "water of life" in the desert of this three-dimensional reality. Moses, one man, drove off all the other herdsmen that had been keeping the maidens from the water (symbolic of all our earthly distractions that keep us from nourishing our spiritual nature). He gave water to the seven maidens and their flocks. Then the girls told him a secret: they are the daughters of a high priest. He then went with them to the tent of the high priest and, ultimately, married the eldest maiden (the highest spiritual center). After these activities, he finally met God in a burning bush. Being predominantly external beings, we interpret this bush to symbolize something outside of ourselves. But consider that the burning bush may represent our own heads, the "bush" of our hair, under which is the crown chakra. This fits so well with Elijah's experience of God within him. It also fits with how the Holy Spirit manifested upon the holy women and disciples as tongues of flame on top of their heads, above the crown chakra.

Once Moses had made contact with God, he was instructed how to transform his staff into a serpent and to then raise up that serpent. (Exodus 2-4) Later in this story, having led all the people into the desert with him, Moses was directed by God to place a "fiery" serpent upon a raised staff so that everyone who looked upon it would be healed. (Numbers 21:8-9) Here again the writer is trying to convey more than a literal, physical story. We see how the serpent can be both poisonous and healing. The one that crawls on the ground is poisonous and deadly, but when the serpent is raised up and "fiery," it is healing. We have to go back to the Garden of Eden to fully understand this, because not only did Adam and Eve fall in the Garden, the serpent fell also. Since we know the serpent symbolizes both the life force and consciousness, this energy can be manifested in earthly ways or heavenly ones. In the teachings of Patanjali and Cayce (EC 264-19 Q & A 13; also see 262-87 Q & A 10, and 444-2 Q & A 23 & 24), the life force within the body can lower or raise our vibrations and consciousness. Moses's story teaches that the kundalini energy within us must be raised up in order for us to commune with God, for God's natural condition is a higher vibration and consciousness than we normally experience.

The process of raising the energy begins with an understanding of where the energy is in the body, how it is raised, and the path it follows through the body. According to the Yoga Sutras, the energy is "coiled" like a serpent (*kundalini*) in the lower part of the torso. It moves up the spinal column (*sushumna*) through the spiritual centers—chakras (wheels) and *padmas* (lotuses)—to the base of the brain and over through the brain to the brow. The path of the kundalini through the body is represented by a cobra in the striking position or by a shepherd's crook (a staff with a large hook on the upper end, flared out at the very tip).

Many books today teach that the kundalini culminates at the crown of the head, but the more ancient images and teachings, as well as Edgar Cayce's, always depict it culminating at the forehead. This will cause some confusion to those who have for years studied and practiced using the crown chakra as the highest spiritual center in the body. Cayce insisted that the true path of the kundalini comes over and through the crown chakra, unites with the Infinite, and then flows into the third-eye chakra in the frontal lobe of the human brain. But let's not allow this difference to become a stumbling block. If you have had much success with the crown chakra as the highest and final awakening, then so be it.

The seven spiritual centers are connected with the seven endocrine glands within the human body: (1) the root chakra and lotus connect with the testes in males, and the ovaries in females, (2) the navel chakra and lotus with the Leydig cells, (3) the solar plexus with the adrenals, (4) the heart with the thymus gland, (5) the throat with the thyroid, (6) the crown with the pineal, and (7) the third eye with the pituitary and the hypothalamus. They are also connected with major nerve ganglia, or plexuses, along the spine: pelvic or lumbar, hypogastric or abdominal, epigastric or solar, cardiac or heart, pharyngeal or throat, and the brain itself.

Patanjali The Yoga Sutra:
- Chakras (physical energy zones associated with the endocrine glands)
- Lotuses (mental thought-clusters)
- Sushumna (the cerebrospinal nervous system of the brain and spinal cord with extended nerves throughout the body)
- Ida and Pingala (the autonomic nervous system, composed of the sympathetic and parasympathetic systems)

The kundalini is historically depicted as a raise serpent, often a serpent with wings. An Egyptian and a Mayan secret of how our human form contains the elan vital or life force in the form of a coiled serpent as in kundalini, and how the mind, symbolized by the wings, raises this energy. The kundalini runs through our two nervous system: the cerebrospinal and the autonomic. The cerebrospinal is the brain and spinal column (the sushumna in yoga). The autonamic is the sympathetic and parasympathetic nervous system (the ida and pingala in yoga). Along these pathways are the seven main endocrine glands, which correlate to the chakras and seven thought-clusters or shaping-concepts symbolized as lotuses. As the energy rises, the spiritual centers are awakened and help to raise the vibrations of the body, illuminate the mind, and free the soul to travel to higher levels of consciousness, even into the presence of the Infinite Eternal (Ein Sof).

This diagram depicts the passage from finite individualness to infinite universalness, or from oneself to oneness with God, the Infinite Eternal. It reveals how we must move from a point of self-consciousness upward and expanding into God consciousness—God being naturally infinite and universal, within which the entire cosmos and all that is in it is contained.

Steps & Stages:
1. Remove all your earthly concerns, the earthly portions of your being and your personality;
2. . Subjugate control to your Soul-self and your Subconscious mind;
3. Feel an openness in your body-temple and a shift toward deeper breathing;
4. Give a strong suggestion to your Subconscious:"Arise my soul, and enter into the Infinite, Universal Mind of God;
5. Use your "imaginative forces" to feel yourself rising and expanding out of finite individualness into infinite universalness and God's natural presence;
6. As you sense God's Presence, connect with it, hold on, plug in—then become receptive, allowing the Infinite to flow into the finite.
7. When it is time to return, rebalance body, mind, and spirit.

This is a list of the sequence of activities that move us from finite individualness to infinite universalness and God's presence. Once connected to the Infinite Eternal (Ein Sof), we are to avoid attempting to tell God how best this should unfold, but allow God to do the magic as He/She knows best. It helps to use the directive: "Not my will, but Thy will." And then feel the Infinite flowing into the finite. A oneness develops, changing our body, mind, and soul for the better. This is an excellent way to spiritualize body, mind, and soul. It is important to rebalance the body, mind, and soul after the meditation has concluded. Otherwise, you'll leave supercharged energy in the upper portions of the body and the mind will be a little "spacey." Equally distribute the energy throughout the body: all the organs, all the bones and muscles, from the top of the head to the tips of the toes and fingers: "equally distribute the energy throughout the body for normal functioning in this world."

I have written a whole book on this amazing process titled, *Passage in Consciousness*, available on Amazon or at my website.

For a deeper study of Kabbalah with Edgar Cayce's helpful perspectives, you may want to read my book *Edgar Cayce and the Kabbalah: A Resource for Soulful Living*. It goes into much more detail because it is 302 pages long. It is available on Amazon.com.

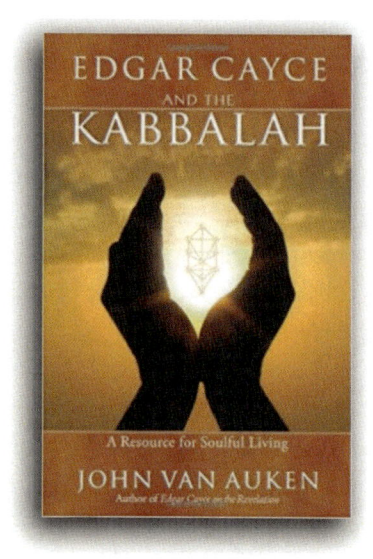

Living in the Light
P.O. Box 4942
Virginia Beach VA 23454 USA
Other books are available at my website as well as a newsletter:
JohnVanAuken.com

Kabbalah.VanAuken@Gmail.com

Made in the USA
Middletown, DE
12 September 2024